MW00559411

SUNDERLAND VS U-BOAT

Bay of Biscay 1943–44

MARK LARDAS

OSPREY PUBLISHING
Bloomsbury Publishing Plc
Kemp House, Chawley Park, Cumnor Hill, Oxford OX2 9PH, UK
1385 Broadway, 5th Floor, New York, NY 10018, USA
E-mail: info@ospreypublishing.com
www.ospreypublishing.com

OSPREY is a trademark of Osprey Publishing Ltd

First published in Great Britain in 2023

© Osprey Publishing Ltd, 2023

All rights reserved. No part of this publication may be reproduced or
transmitted in any form or by any means, electronic or mechanical, including
photocopying, recording, or any information storage or retrieval system,
without prior permission in writing from the publishers.

A catalogue record for this book is available from the British Library.

ISBN: PB 9781472854810; eBook 9781472854803; ePDF 9781472854827;
XML 9781472854797

23 24 25 26 27 10 9 8 7 6 5 4 3 2 1

Edited by Tony Holmes
Cover artwork, battlescene, three-views, cockpit, Engaging the Enemy and
armament views by Jim Laurier
Map and tactical diagram by www.bounford.com
Index by Angela Hall
Typeset by PDQ Digital Media Solutions, Bungay, UK
Printed and bound in India by Replika Press Private Ltd.

Osprey Publishing supports the Woodland Trust, the UK's leading woodland
conservation charity.

To find out more about our authors and books visit www.ospreypublishing.com.
Here you will find extracts, author interviews, details of forthcoming events
and the option to sign up for our newsletter.

Author's Dedication

To Vanessa – my nephew John's new bride. Welcome to the family.

Cover Artworks

On 8 August 1943, two Sunderland IIIs (one flown by Flg Off Reader
Hanbury of No. 228 Sqn and the other commanded by Flg Off Irwin A. E.
"Chic" Clarke of No. 461 Sqn) spotted veteran Type IXB U-boat *U-106* on
the surface northwest of Cape Ortegal, Spain. One of the most successful
German submarines of World War II, the U-boat was on its tenth patrol when
the vessel was badly damaged by a depth charge dropped by a Wellington of
No. 407 Sqn on 2 August. Led by Oberleutnant zur see Wolf-Dietrich
Damerow, the crew had attempted to limp back to their base at Lorient on the
surface as the U-boat was unable to dive.

Having spotted their quarry, Hanbury and Clarke circled for a few minutes
before launching a coordinated attack on *U-106* so as to split its potentially
formidable defence. Clarke (in the lower of the two Sunderlands seen in the
cover artworks) attacked the port bow, while Hanbury (some 50ft higher)
dived on the starboard bow. According to Damerow, 'The one to starboard is
engaged by quadruple 2cm, and the one to port by the single 2cm and
machine guns'. Clarke roared in at a height of just 50ft, while his bow gunner,
Sgt John Royal, sprayed *U-106*'s 'bandstands' with 0.303-in. rounds that cut
down the crew of the quad 20mm weapon on the 'Wintergarten' directly aft of
the conning tower.

The two Sunderlands flew directly over *U-106* within seconds of each
other, Clarke dropping six depth charges 50 yards astern of the submarine.
Hanbury, attacking from a height of 100ft, perfectly straddled the vessel with
seven depth charges that bracketed the conning tower. The twin attacks left
U-106 in a desperate condition. According to Damerow, Clarke's depth
charges 'caused severe concussion to the boat', and Hanbury's ripped 'the port
engine-room switchboard from its securings, causing it to catch fire. The
starboard diesel stopped. Thick smoke filled the boat, which listed to port
with a bad leak'. Minutes later *U-106* exploded and sank, taking 22 crew with
it. Damerow and 35 of his men survived, however, being rescued by German
E-boats.

Previous Page

A newly-delivered Sunderland V of No. 201 Sqn, flying from Castle Archdale,
in Northern Ireland, escorts an Atlantic convoy off the southwest coast of
Ireland in February 1945. By then, RAF Coastal Command had all but
defeated the U-boat threat. (Philip Jarrett Collection)

CONTENTS

INTRODUCTION

On 25 March 1943, Type VIIC U-boat *U-230* was completing its first war patrol. At sea 42 days, it attacked convoy SC 121 and sank the 2,868-ton steamship *Egyptian*. The vessel was on its homeward leg, entering the Bay of Biscay and heading to Brest, anticipating the bands and fanfare that greeted successful submarines. Aboard as First Watch Officer was Leutnant Herbert Werner, future author of *Iron Coffins*, on his fourth war patrol. His previous deployments had been on another Type VIIC U-boat, *U-557*, which had sunk five ships totalling more than 28,000 tons while Werner was aboard. He was no stranger to the Bay of Biscay.

This trip was different, however, Werner reporting, 'That night we made three radar contacts. Three times we crash-dived and three times an aircraft dropped a cluster of bombs [almost certainly depth charges] in our wake.' Between 1000 hrs on 24 March and 1430 hrs the following day, *U-230* experienced four more attacks by aircraft, including one by a Sunderland. It dropped four depth charges on the U-boat, but *U-230* escaped damage. Thereafter, its skipper, Kapitänleutnant Paul Siegmann, 'decided to run submerged during the day and to travel on the surface at night only, when the Tommies would be forced to resort to their radar to find us'.

U-230's next war patrol took place between 24 April and 24 May 1943, during RAF Coastal Command's new offensive over the Bay of Biscay. The submarine's return voyage on its second war patrol was the stuff of nightmares. The Kriegsmarine lost 42 U-boats that May, 21 to aircraft attacks. Ten U-boats were sunk in the Bay of Biscay as submarines departed or returned to base. Sunderlands flown by Nos. 201 and 228 Sqns of the Royal Air Force (RAF) and Nos. 10 and 461 Sqns of the Royal Australian Air Force (RAAF) accounted for half of them.

Werner recalled, 'night was no different from the day [in May 1943]. We crash-dived three times, evading 12 more bombs by meagre margins. After dark the next day

we were forced to make six crash-dives, each time receiving the inevitable four charges'. *U-230* managed to escape unscathed, and the U-boat only survived the following night by hiding in a fleet of French fishing trawlers, rendering it invisible to the hunting Sunderlands and Wellingtons. The once mighty U-boat, 'scourge of the Atlantic', had been neutralised by aircraft.

The aircraft most associated with RAF Coastal Command and the Battle of the Atlantic is the Short Sunderland, the four-engined flying boat that entered service with the RAF in 1938. It remained in the RAF Coastal Command inventory until 1959, and served on with the Royal New Zealand Air Force for a further eight years. The Sunderland was the only RAF Coastal Command aircraft to remain a frontline type from September 1939 through to May 1945. When the war in Europe ended, Britain began transferring its Sunderland squadrons in the Atlantic to the Pacific theatre.

The Sunderland was the aircraft most feared by U-boat commanders, and most frequently mentioned in their memoirs. It seemed as if almost every four-engined aircraft they encountered was a Sunderland. The stock cover for any book about RAF Coastal Command shows a Sunderland attacking a U-boat. Yet the Sunderland was not the most numerous multi-engined aircraft involved in the Battle of the Atlantic. Indeed, it was not even the most numerous four-engined aircraft.

At the height of the battle in 1943–44, there were only seven Sunderland squadrons with around 85 aircraft. By contrast, there were 14 Liberator squadrons (half of which were assigned to the USAAF's 479th Anti-Submarine Group or the US Navy's Fleet Air Wing 7) with approximately 220 aircraft in service. RAF Coastal Command also fielded seven Wellington squadrons, five equipped with the Halifax and two Fortress II/III units.

Yet the Sunderland caught the imagination of both sides. Part of the reason was the aircraft's appearance. It was portly, bearing a closer resemblance to 'J. Wellington Wimpy' of *Popeye* fame than did the twin-engined Wellington (nicknamed the 'Wimpy'). The

This became a common sight in 1943–44 – a U-boat breaks the surface after being depth-charged by a Sunderland in the Bay of Biscay. Although the vessel had managed to dive before the flying boat reached it, the depth charges (set to explode at a depth of 25ft below the surface of the water) detonated quickly enough to inflict sufficient damage to force the unidentified U-boat back to the surface. A damaged U-boat was more likely the result of a Sunderland attack than a sunk U-boat. (Author's Collection)

A well-weathered Sunderland III of Canadian-manned No. 422 Sqn patrols the Atlantic off the west coast of Ireland on 15 April 1943. Equipped with the Sunderland III for more than two-and-a-half years, the unit would be credited with a single U-boat sunk (*U-625*) during that period. It also lost a Sunderland to defensive fire (from *U-448*). (Tony Holmes Collection)

Sunderland's appearance made it look solid, reliable and steady, the embodiment of the British spirit. The men that flew in it loved the aircraft. Sgt G. D. Williams of No. 228 Sqn said of it after the war, 'The Sunderland was the best aircraft ever built, being thoroughly reliable and easy to live with in the air or on the water.' Few U-boat crews spoke as enthusiastically of their vessels either during or after the war.

The Sunderland also captured the imagination of the public during the early war years. Just two weeks into the conflict, a pair of Sunderlands rescued the crew of a sinking British freighter. It was also credited with the first two confirmed kills of U-boats by RAF Coastal Command aircraft. One of the first Sunderland units committed to the Battle of the Atlantic was the RAAF No. 10 Sqn, which had been in Britain converting to the aircraft when war broke out in Europe in September 1939. It duly became a magnet for press coverage, a symbol of Commonwealth unity and a point of pride for Australia.

Most importantly, the Sunderland was a U-boat killer. Once equipped with weapons that worked, the aircraft lived up to its press coverage. Despite never having the best U-boat hunting tools in RAF Coastal Command, the Sunderland racked up an impressive total of submarine kills in 1943–44. In many ways the Sunderland was to the U-boat what the U-boat was to the merchant vessel – the ultimate predator. U-boats would strike a convoy unseen, sometimes from within its defensive perimeter of escorting warships. If all went well, having torpedoed several vessels, the U-boat would slip away unseen, leaving death and destruction behind it. Sometimes the submarine was caught making its attack and had to battle its way out.

Similarly, the Sunderland would sweep out of the sky, often unseen, to rain high explosives on an unwary U-boat. When all went well, it too slipped away unscathed, leaving destruction in its wake. There was even a similarity in the outcome of their attacks. Often, the U-boat and Sunderland would miss their prey, despite making a near-perfect attack. Sometimes they missed because they were over-hasty. Chance always played a role. In both cases vigilance by the attacker was required to ensure success, and vigilance by the defender could foil an attack. It is that knife-edge balance that make the duels between Sunderlands and U-boats so fascinating.

CHRONOLOGY

1933
November — RAF issues Specification R.2/33 for a four-engined maritime patrol seaplane.

1934
October — Short Brothers decides to bid on R.2/33, developing a design that becomes the Sunderland.

1935
21 May — Kriegsmarine is formed.
18 June — Anglo-German Naval Treaty signed, permitting Germany to build U-boats.
29 June — Kriegsmarine commissions *U-1*, its first U-boat since the end of World War I.

1936
14 July — RAF Coastal Command is established
12 August — *U-27*, first Type VII U-boat, commissioned.

1937
14 October — The prototype Sunderland, K4774, makes its first flight.

1938
21 April — The first production Sunderland I (75 built) completes its maiden flight.
28 May — RAF accepts the first Sunderland for active duty.

Few RAF Coastal Command aircraft were as storied or famous as the Sunderland (here, Mk I P9604 from No. 10 Sqn, taxiing out at Oban, in Scotland, in August 1940). It was popular among its crews, familiar to the British public due to its unique appearance, and a nightmare throughout the war to Germany's U-bootsmanner. Indeed, they saw a Sunderland in every attacking aircraft. (Author's Collection)

1939
3 September — Britain and France declare war on Germany.
18 September — Two Sunderlands rescue the 34 crew of the merchantman SS *Kensington Court*, sunk by a U-boat.

1940
30 January — First U-boat kill credited to RAF Coastal Command. A No. 228 Sqn Sunderland forces previously-damaged *U-55* to scuttle.
May — Mk I air-to-surface vessel (ASV) radar enters operation.
22 June — France surrenders. Germany occupies northern France and its maritime provinces, whose ports will soon be home to U-boats.

1 July	*U-26* scuttled after depth charging by the corvette HMS *Gladiolus* and bombs from No. 10 Sqn Sunderland.
7 July	U-boats begin operating out of French Atlantic ports, with the arrival of U-30 at Lorient.
September	Construction of first French U-boat pens completed.
October	ASV Mk I installed in 25 Sunderlands.

1941

1 January	Sunderlands sent to Iceland.
15 January	Sunderlands sent to Freetown, in Sierra Leone.
23 January	Production of the 250lb Mk VIII depth charge commences.
May	Barrier search patrols initiated in Bay of Biscay and Britain/Iceland/Faroe Islands gap.
June	1. *Flotille* transfers to Brest.
August	Sunderland II (43 built) enters service.
October	ASV Mk II radar installed in Sunderlands.
December	Sunderland III (461 built) enters service.

1942

August	FuMB1 (better known as Metox after its French manufacturer) radar detector introduced to U-boats, this system warning crews via an audio alert when its antenna detected high frequency radio transmissions from an Allied aircraft's ASV Mk II radar.

1943

February	Air Marshal Sir John Slessor becomes commander-in-chief, RAF Coastal Command.
20 March	Air Marshal Slessor orders RAF Coastal Command to commence the Bay Offensive (specifically targeting U-boats in Bay of Biscay) the following month.

April	ASV Mk III becomes available to Sunderland squadrons.
2 May	*U-405* sunk by a Sunderland of No. 461 Sqn in Bay of Biscay.
8 May	*U-663* sunk by a Sunderland of No. 10 Sqn in Bay of Biscay.
13 May	*U-775* sunk by HMCS *Drumheller*, HMS *Lagen* and a Sunderland of No. 423 Sqn in North Atlantic.
24 May	Großadmiral Karl Dönitz withdraws U-boats from the North Atlantic.
24 May	*U-441* shoots down a Sunderland of No. 228 Sqn in Bay of Biscay. First kill by Flak from a U-boat.
31 May	In two separate Bay of Biscay incidents, *U-440* is sunk by a Sunderland of No. 201 Sqn and *U-563* is sunk by a combined attack from a Halifax of No. 58 Sqn and two Sunderlands from Nos. 10 and 228 Sqns.
13 June	Sunderland of No. 228 Sqn encounters five U-boats (*U-185*, *U-358*, *U-564*, *U-634* and *U-653*) in Bay of Biscay and is shot down by Flak from all five vessels.
13 July	*U-607* sunk by a Sunderland of No. 228 Sqn in Bay of Biscay.
30 July	*U-461* sunk by a Sunderland of No. 461 Sqn in Bay of Biscay.
July	Ju 88s begin long-range fighter sweeps in Bay of Biscay, attempting to drive off RAF Coastal Command aircraft.
1 August	In a battle off Cape Finisterre, in Spain, between *U-454* and a No.10 Sqn Sunderland, the U-boat is sunk and the flying boat shot down.
1 August	In separate incidents in Bay of Biscay, *U-383* is sunk by a Sunderland from No. 228 Sqn and *U-454* is sunk by a Sunderland from No. 10 Sqn.
2 August	*U-106* sunk by two Sunderlands from Nos. 228 and 461 Sqns just west of Bay of Biscay.

3 August	Use of Metox ordered suspended by U-boat headquarters.
4 August	*U-489* is sunk and a No. 423 Sqn Sunderland shot down in a battle between the two fought in the Iceland/Britain gap.
8 October	*U-610* sunk by a Sunderland of No. 423 west of Ireland.
17 October	*U-448* shoots down a Sunderland of No. 422 Sqn when attacked in central North Atlantic.

The Type IXB U-boat *U-106* returns to 2. *Flotille's* home port of Lorient following a patrol in early 1943. Credited with sinking 22 ships in ten patrols, the submarine was sunk by Sunderlands on 2 August 1943. (Getty Images)

1944

8 January	*U-426* sunk by a Sunderland of No. 10 Sqn west of Bay of Biscay.
28 January	*U-571* sunk by a Sunderland of No. 461 Sqn west of Ireland.
10 March	*U-625* sunk by a Sunderland of No. 422 Sqn west of Ireland.
24 May	*U-675* sunk by a Sunderland of No. 4 (Coastal) Operational Training Unit (OTU) in Norwegian Sea.
7 June	*U-955* sunk by a Sunderland of No. 201 Sqn in Bay of Biscay.
8 June	*U-970* sunk by a Sunderland of No. 228 Sqn in Bay of Biscay.
11 June	In separate incidents, *U-333* and *U-228* are attacked by Sunderlands, and they shoot down their attackers. Both aircraft were from No. 228 Sqn.
12 June	*U-333* is attacked by a Sunderland of No. 201 Sqn and shoots it down.
8 July	*U-243* sunk by a Sunderland of No. 10 Sqn in Bay of Biscay.
11 July	*U-1222* sunk by a Sunderland of No. 201 Sqn in Bay of Biscay.
7 August	Brest abandoned as a U-boat base.

11 August	*U-385* sunk by a Sunderland of No. 461 Sqn in Bay of Biscay
13 August	*U-270* sunk by a Sunderland of No. 461 Sqn in Bay of Biscay.
18 August	*U-107* sunk by a Sunderland of No. 201 Sqn in Bay of Biscay.
30 August	First flight of prototype Sunderland IV (later renamed Seaford due to significant airframe changes – ten built).
September 23	Last U-boat leaves a French port on an operational mission.
November 25	*U-482* sunk by HMS *Ascension* after being located by a Sunderland of No. 330 Sqn west of the Shetland Islands.

1945

February	Sunderland V enters service (155 built and 33 Mk IIIs upgraded to Mk V specification).
30 April	Dönitz succeeds Adolf Hitler as Head of State of the Third Reich.
8 May	Germany surrenders, ending the war in Europe (and the Battle of the Atlantic).

DESIGN AND DEVELOPMENT

SHORT SUNDERLAND

Britain's armed forces embraced seaplanes at the same time as they began flying heavier-than-air craft. When the Royal Naval Air Service (RNAS) was formally established on 1 July 1914, the first aircraft it obtained were seaplanes. For an island nation with substantial maritime responsibilities, aircraft landing on water were natural fits. They were ideal for maritime patrol, and seaplanes did not need runways, only a sheltered patch of water such as an estuary, bay or lake. Furthermore, if mechanical problems or weather forced seaplanes down in open water, the crew had a chance of survival.

Although seaplanes worked best when operating from a shore facility that provided workshops and sheltered storage, they could be serviced by tenders – ships equipped with maintenance workshops, armament storage and fuelling facilities. You could establish a seaplane base anywhere a ship could steam, setting it up overnight.

There were two types of seaplanes – floatplanes and flying boats. A floatplane used either a single large float or a pair of floats for buoyancy. A flying boat had a hull-like fuselage that floated on the water. The floatplane's advantage was you could convert any land-based aircraft into a floatplane by replacing landing gear with floats. Its disadvantage was the float created significant drag when airborne and the floats'

weight reduced the payload the aircraft could carry. This dramatically reduced performance.

A flying boat had the float built into the hull, reducing airborne drag and structural weight. Although typically it could not match a landplane in respect to speed and manoeuvrability, a flying boat performed significantly better than a similarly-sized floatplane. This was especially true of multi-engined designs used for maritime patrol. Virtually all multi-engined seaplanes to see service with the RNAS and the Royal Flying Corps (RFC), and their successor, the RAF, were flying boats. During the 1920s and early 1930s, the RAF filled its maritime patrol squadrons with multi-engined biplane flying boats. By 1935 it wanted something more modern and more powerful. The result was the Sunderland.

Shorts developed the aircraft in parallel with its Empire flying boat, destined for service as a commercial airliner. Both were high-wing, four-engined aircraft of all-metal construction that shared a superficially similar appearance. The prototype Sunderland even used the same Bristol Pegasus X radial engines as the production Empire. Nevertheless, they were independent designs. The Empire was developed to meet the requirements of Imperial Airways for an airliner capable of crossing the Atlantic. The Sunderland was a response to Air Ministry Specification R.2/33 issued in 1933. It sought an aircraft with equal performance to the one-off Short Sarafand, a long-range flying boat designed in the late 1920s and delivered to the RAF in 1932.

When built, the Sarafand had the distinction of being the largest aircraft in Britain, and it relied on no fewer than six 850hp Rolls-Royce Buzzard engines housed in three tractor/pusher nacelles between the wings to get it aloft. Like smaller contemporary RAF flying boats the Saro London and Supermarine Stranraer, the Sarafand was a biplane that made extensive use of fabric to cover its wings and tail surfaces. Again like the Stranraer and London, the Sarafand had an anodised Alclad (aluminium) fuselage.

Sunderland prototype K4774, which first flew on 14 October 1937, was photographed on the slipway outside Short's Rochester factory on the River Medway just prior to its maiden flight. (Philip Jarrett Collection)

The Sunderland's distinctive anodised aluminium hull dominates this near head-on view of K4774. The flying boat had a broad transverse 'V' shape that came to a knife-edge at the end of the planing surface. A keel ran the length of the hull, and it had a discontinuous 'step' located under the wing (visible here just forward of the beaching gear). Aft of the step, the hull was shallower. (Philip Jarrett Collection)

The RAF retained biplanes longer than most other air forces, and the R.2/33 specification did not require manufacturers to submit a monoplane design. It called for a long-range general purpose flying boat with a range of at least 1,260 nautical miles, a top speed of 150mph and a cruising speed of 130mph – all performance statistics that matched those of the Sarafand. Four engines were specified, but the design could either be monoplane or biplane.

Shorts had been building seaplanes since 1911, some seven years before the formation of the RAF. Its first flying boat design had taken to the air in 1917, and during the interwar years, the Kent-based company became a major supplier of flying boats to both airlines and the RAF. While it pushed ahead on the design of the Empire flying boat (Imperial Airways was in a hurry to get hold of it), Shorts dawdled on development of its R.2/33-inspired aircraft due to a lack of urgency by the RAF. In October 1934, nearly a year after the Air Ministry had issued its specification, Shorts finally responded with what eventually became the Sunderland – an all-metal, high-wing monoplane with four engines.

The aircraft was an order of magnitude better than any previous British military flying boat. It had a cruising speed and top speed 40 per cent faster than any RAF seaplane then in service, whilst the aircraft's range of 1,550 nautical miles was significantly greater than the specification demanded. The flying boat could carry up to 24,000lb of bombs, fuel and crew, and stay airborne for 13 hours. It was also heavily armed. The design called for a 37mm gun in the nose, two 0.303-in. waist guns and a single 0.303-in. gun in the tail.

By the time the Sunderland went into production, its armament had been altered to twin 0.303-in. guns in a powered turret in the nose, four 0.303-in. guns in a powered turret in the tail and two hand-held 0.303-in. Vickers 'K' guns in the waist. Prior to the Sunderland's introduction into service, preceding RAF flying boats had been armed with only three or four clip-fed 0.303-in. Lewis guns – rifle-calibre machine guns dating back to World War I.

The Air Ministry liked what it saw, issuing Shorts with a contract to build a prototype, which the company duly designated the S.25. The Air Ministry also issued a similar contract to Saunders-Roe (Saro), intending to conduct a fly-off between the

An early-production Sunderland I motors along the Medway in 1938. The aircraft lacks any armament, this being installed by the RAF following its acceptance for operational service. (Philip Jarrett Collection)

two designs. Saro's response was the A.33, although the aircraft never made it as far as a fly-off. The prototype suffered structural failure during pre-release testing and was written off before the competition could take place.

It really did not matter, for Short's design was clearly superior. The parasol-winged A.33 was slower than the S.25, with a shorter endurance and less powerful engines. Smaller, lighter and clearly structurally weaker, it could only carry 40 per cent of the S.25's payload. When the A.33 proved unable to compete, the Air Ministry awarded the contract to Shorts. It had a flying prototype that exceeded all specification requirements.

Prototype K4774 was completed on 14 October 1937. The aircraft was designed to be fitted with 1,010hp Pegasus XXII engines, but these were unavailable at the time so 950hp Pegasus Xs were temporarily fitted – as previously noted, these engines were used by the Empire flying boats, so Shorts had plenty on hand. The prototype flew two days later, on 16 October, completing two flights that day. After a week of flight testing, the prototype was grounded so that a series of upgrades, including the installation of its Pegasus XXII engines, could be carried out. The turret armament was changed, too, with the 37mm cannon in the nose being replaced by twin 0.303-in. machine guns in a powered turret.

The fitting of the turrets fore and aft in the prototype significantly shifted the flying boat's centre of gravity aft. To compensate, Shorts swept the wings back 4.25 degrees. It also moved the 'step' – a break in the hull ahead of which the aircraft 'rode' when taking off from water – further back. This pushed the pivot point aft, allowing the Sunderland to lift its tail out of the water earlier and facilitating take-off. While the wings were swept back, the engine nacelles were kept perpendicular to the leading edge. This left the engines canted slightly outward, rather like an eighteenth-century duckfoot pistol.

The result of all these changes turned the S.25 prototype into the Sunderland I. The flying boat entered production in early 1938 at Shorts' Rochester factory in Kent, and the first examples were issued to the RAF's No. 210 Sqn in June of that same year. When World War II began, the RAF had accepted 40 Sunderland Is, but only nine were operational in combat squadrons of RAF Coastal Command. The rest were

SUNDERLAND III

85ft 4in.

32ft 10.5in.

112ft 9.5in.

assigned elsewhere in the Empire or with units that were working up.

The Sunderland was not designed as an anti-submarine warfare (ASW) aircraft; it was a general-purpose maritime patrol aircraft. The flying boat was intended to scout out the enemy fleet, intercept it and, if necessary, destroy shipping. The Sunderland possessed anti-submarine capabilities, however, and it eventually became one of World War II's premier ASW platforms, but it was not optimised for that.

The Sunderland's size made it a formidable aircraft. The flying boat could carry a large crew in comfort, with bunks for off-duty personnel to rest in and a galley for meals. This allowed crew rotation, reducing fatigue. It carried up to 2,000lb of bombs, depth charges or mines. However, as a flying boat, it lacked a bomb-bay. Munitions were stored in a bomb room alongside the wings. When needed, they were loaded on to underwing racks, which then traversed out between the fuselage and inboard engines to be dropped.

The Sunderland was not the ideal ASW aircraft, being relatively slow and a large target. Indeed, the flying boat's approach was 'stately'. It could not swoop in quickly on a U-boat. Nevertheless, the Sunderland was good enough, and until the Mk VIII depth charge appeared in January 1941, it was the only modern RAF Coastal Command aircraft capable of carrying the 450lb Mk VII airborne depth charge – this was the only RAF weapon that could reliably sink a U-boat. Although Sunderlands lacked the range to reach the central Atlantic, when operating from bases in Cornwall and Devon they could patrol as far south as Cape Ortegal, on Spain's northern coast. That made the aircraft invaluable during the Bay campaigns of 1942–43.

The Sunderland I was built between early 1938 and August 1941, and in that time only 90 were produced – 75 by Shorts at Rochester and 15 under license by Blackburn. Production was slow because Shorts was also building the Stirling (the RAF's first four-engined heavy bomber), which had higher priority. Sunderland production was never high. Thousands of Lancaster and Halifax four-engined bombers were built, and tens of thousands of Liberators, while just 777 Sunderlands were completed. This was principally because the flying boat was never intended for mass production, being seen as a specialised maritime aircraft and, therefore, having limited operational potential according to the Air Ministry. Yet the Sunderland remained in production throughout the war, with the final example being delivered in June 1946.

The aircraft experienced significant growth during its career, with five different variants being built. Each one had successively more powerful engines culminating with four 1,200hp Pratt & Whitney R-1830 Twin Wasp radials fitted to the Sunderland V. Increased engine power also meant that the aircraft could carry the additional weight associated with the flying boat's improved capabilities. A key addition to the Sunderland was ASV Mk II radar, which was installed as standard from

The cockpit of the Sunderland barely altered in appearance during the flying boat's eight-year production run. The captain of the aircraft would occupy the left seat, with the first pilot sat alongside him. Note the rudimentary ring and bead gunsight mounted on the instrument coaming ahead of the captain's position. (Philip Jarrett Collection)

OPPOSITE

Sunderland III EJ133 was the third aircraft in a batch of 15 built by Shorts in Rochester between April and December 1942. Equipped with ASV Mk III and three powered turrets, the aircraft was issued to No. 119 Sqn as part of the unit's transition from the Catalina IIA to the Sunderland III at Pembroke Dock in the autumn of 1942. When No. 119 Sqn disbanded in April of the following year, EJ133 was passed on to No. 461 Sqn, recently arrived at Pembroke Dock from Hamworthy Junction (Poole Harbour), in Dorset. The Sunderland served with the Australian unit until December 1944, when it was damaged beyond repair after it hit a tender upon landing at Pembroke Dock.

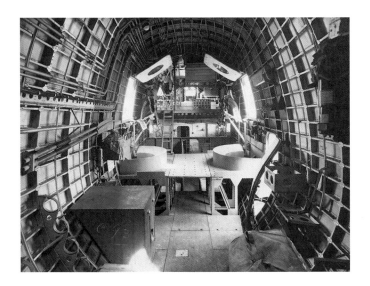

October 1941 – a first for an RAF Coastal Command aircraft. Progressively heavier defensive armament was added, with the Sunderland II featuring a powered dorsal turret.

By war's end, the Sunderland had become the RAF's most effective flying boat, synonymous with the Allied victory over the U-boat menace.

U-BOAT

This interior view of a Sunderland V, looking forward, reveals just how deep the fuselage was. Its broad cross section was sufficiently ample to house two decks forward. The mid-fuselage windows are seen open here, with the single 0.303-in. machine guns in their mountings that fired through these openings in the stowed position. The mid-fuselage weapons were not present on the early marks of Sunderland. The hatch to the right of the ladder led to the wardroom and, beyond the latter, the mooring compartment with its anchor and winch. (Philip Jarrett Collection)

The Kriegsmarine deployed four types of U-boat in 1943, namely the VII, IX, X and XIV designs. The pre-war Type IA and II were active in the Atlantic and North Sea from 1939 through to 1941. A few U-boats in the Kriegsmarine during this period had been built for foreign navies prior to being pressed into German service when World War II started, or had been captured from conquered nations. By 1942 all of these 'acquired' vessels had either been sunk or withdrawn for training or combat service in the Baltic or Black Seas. All designs were improved versions of German U-boats from World War I, including the submarines engaged by RAF Coastal Command from September 1939 through to the Biscay campaign of 1942–43.

Although Germany had suffered a humiliating defeat in November 1918, it ended the conflict with a reputation for building the world's best submarines. Furthermore, its Kaiserliche Marine (Imperial German Navy) operated them more effectively than any other nation. U-boats raised such concern that the Treaty of Versailles, which ended World War I, expressly forbade Germany from building and operating U-boats. Despite this, from 1922 through to 1943, its U-boat designers borrowed heavily from submarines that saw service in World War I. Not until 1943 did Kriegsmarine naval architects design a new, radically-better U-boat.

Germany had commenced building submarines in 1903. The Kaiserliche Marine duly purchased its first U-boat, the *U-1*, in 1906. Four years later, *U-19* entered service. Displacing 640 tons surfaced and 824 tons submerged, it was 64.1m in length, had a six-metre beam and a height of 7.3m. The vessel had a test depth of 50m and a surfaced range of 9,700 nautical miles. *U-19*, which could reach 15.4 knots surfaced and 9.5 knots submerged, carried ten 50cm torpedoes, which could be fired from two tubes forward and two aft. It had three deck guns – one 105mm, one 88mm and one 37mm. The submarine was powered by two MAN eight-cylinder diesel engines producing 1,700hp, which in turn powered two AEG electric motors generating 1,184shp. *U-19* would serve as the template for all subsequent U-boats through to 1943.

By the end of World War I, Imperial Germany had two U-boat types analogous to World War II's Type VII and Type IX vessels which formed the backbone of the Kriegsmarine's U-boat force. These were the UB III and Type 93 classes. The UB IIIs were effectively Type VII boats, but only two-thirds their size. With an overall length of 55.3m and a maximum breadth of 5.8m, they displaced 516 tons surfaced and 651 tons submerged (the pressure hull was 40.1m long, with a 3.9m diameter). Manned by a crew of 35, the UB III had five torpedo tubes (four forward and one aft), ten torpedoes and an 88mm deck gun with 160 rounds. It had a maximum speed of 13.6 knots surfaced and eight knots submerged. With a range of 9,040 nautical miles at six knots and a test depth of 75m, the UB III was a very capable submarine.

The Type 93-class U-boats were downscaled Kriegsmarine Type IX vessels. Ocean-going submarines intended for Atlantic patrols, they displaced 838 tons surfaced, 1,000 tons submerged and were 71.55m long with a 6.3m beam (the pressure hull was 56m long, with a 4.15m diameter). With a crew of 39, the submarine had six torpedo tubes (four bow, two stern), 16 torpedoes and a 105mm deck gun with 140 rounds. It had a range of 9,000 nautical miles surfaced at eight knots, with a maximum speed of 16.8 knots surfaced and 8.6 knots submerged.

The Reichsmarine (which replaced the Kaiserliche Marine after World War I) established the *Ingenieurskantoor voor Scheepsbow* (IvS) – a submarine design office – in the Dutch city of The Hague in 1922. Although the IvS was supposedly a commercial company so as to evade the Versailles Treaty's limitations on designing U-boats, it was in reality funded by the Reichsmarine. IvS designed and sold submarines for export. Turkey was its first customer, buying two vessels that were upgrades of the UB III design. Christened *Birinci İnönü* and *İkinci İnönü*, they were built in Rotterdam and delivered in 1928.

IvS soon went beyond updating World War I designs, however, creating three new U-boat types between 1927 and 1933 that were subsequently used by the Kriegsmarine

The rear fuselage of the Sunderland tapered up until it ended at the Nash & Thompson FN 11 tail turret, the entrance to which is obscured by the crewman heading aft in this photograph. (Philip Jarrett Collection)

UB III-class vessels *UB-86* (in the foreground) and *UB-112* lay off Castle Beach, near Falmouth in Cornwall, in 1921. These submarines were amongst six captured U-boats used in explosives trials off the Cornish coast in November–December 1920, with the Admiralty testing for weaknesses in their construction. All bar one of these vessels were UB IIIs (on which the highly successful Type VII boats of World War II would be based) that had been surrendered to the Allies at Harwich, in Essex, in November 1918 in accordance with the requirements of the Armistice. (NHHC)

The Type 93-class U-boat *U-110* completed three patrols and sank ten ships totalling 26,963 tons prior to being depth-charged and sunk off the northwest coast of Ireland on 15 March 1918. An ocean-going U-boat, the Type 93-class vessel was effectively a downscaled Type IX, almost 200 of which would equip the Kriegsmarine in World War II. (NHHC)

in World War II. The first was built by Spain in 1929–30, the *Submarino E-1* being an oceangoing vessel intended for long-range independent patrols. The design re-emerged in Germany in 1936 as the Type IA U-boat. Only two were built (*U-25* and *U-26*), while an upgraded version became the Type IX U-boat. *E-1* never served in the *Armada Española*, being sold to Turkey in 1935 and serving as *Gür* until 1947. Finland, newly independent from the former Russian Empire after World War I and needing a navy, ordered the next two IvS designs. One design, commissioned in Finland as *Vesikko*, served as the prototype for the Type II coastal U-boat. The other, the *Vetehinen*-class, became the prototype for the Type VII U-boat.

Germany duly had plans ready for three different U-boats when it rejected the Treaty of Versailles in 1936. The Type II U-boat ceased production in 1941, the Type IA evolved into the Type IX and the Type VII would remain in production through 1944.

The Type II boats were smallest, displacing 254 tons surfaced and 303 tons submerged. By August 1939 they were being relegated to a training role, playing no part in the Battle of the Atlantic after 1941. More than 690 Type VIIs and nearly 200 Type IXs were commissioned during World War II. The Type VIIs displaced between 626 and 770 tons surfaced and 775 and 871 tons submerged (depending on the variant). They had five torpedo tubes, four forward and one aft. The Type IX displaced between 1,032 and 1,616 tons surfaced and 1,152 and 1,804 tons submerged, again depending on the variant.

The Kriegsmarine developed designs for two other U-boats prior to World War II, the Type X and Type XI. The Type X was a minelaying U-boat, and it was significantly larger than other German submarines. The original Type X would have displaced 2,500 tons submerged, and had dry storage for mines. The Type XA added extra mine

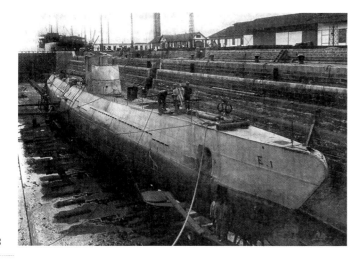

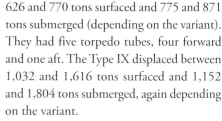

The Spanish-built Submarino *E-1*, designed by the IvS, was effectively the prototype of the German Type IA U-boat. It is seen here under construction in Cadiz. (Public Domain)

storage shafts in the saddle tanks. Neither went into production. A slightly downscaled version, the Type XB, was built from 1939, however, the vessel displacing 1,735 tons surfaced and 2,177 tons submerged. Featuring two stern torpedo tubes and 30 mine shafts, it could carry 15 torpedoes and 66 mines.

The even-larger Type XI was intended as a long-range raider. With a submerged displacement of 4,650 tons, as designed it had six torpedo tubes (four forward and two aft), two twin 128mm gun turrets (one forward of the conning tower and one aft) and a hangar for a single-seat parasol-wing Arado Ar 231 collapsible floatplane. Contracts for four were awarded in January 1939, but they were cancelled nine months later upon the outbreak of war.

The Type XI had a World War I counterpart. In 1916, Germany launched *Deutschland*, an unarmed civilian-flagged cargo submarine. It was intended to run strategic materials, such as rubber, past the British blockade of Germany. Displacing 1,488 tons surfaced and 1,875 tons submerged, the vessel was only slightly smaller than the Type XB. Downsized, it became the basis for a dedicated supply U-boat, the Type XIV. Larger than the XB, it displaced 1,932 tons surfaced and up to 2,300 tons submerged. Devoid of torpedo tubes, the Type XIV enjoyed a modest production run that resulted in the completion of just ten examples.

One limitation that affected both the Type VII and early Type IXs was their poor range, which meant that they were unable to perform truly oceanic operations.

A pre-war photograph of Type VIIA U-boat *U-36*. The Type VII, built in seven variants, served as the backbone of the Kriegsmarine's U-boat force from the late 1930s through to war's end. Nearly 1,000 were ordered and 703 completed, making the Type VII the most produced submarine class in history. *U-36* was torpedoed by the Royal Navy submarine HMS *Salmon* on 4 December 1939 whilst surfaced near the Norwegian port of Stavanger. All 40 crew perished. (NHHC)

U-464 was one of just ten Type XIV U-boats commissioned by the Kriegsmarine in 1940–43, its function being to supply food, fuel and torpedoes at sea to the short-range Type VII boats. Due to their small numbers, Type XIVs were a prized target for RAF Coastal Command during the Battle of the Bay. *U-464* was scuttled by its crew on 20 August 1942, just six days into its first patrol, after the vessel had been badly damaged in an attack by a US Navy PBY Catalina from VP-73 southeast of Iceland. All but two of its 54-man crew survived, being rescued by an Icelandic trawler. (NHHC)

U-106

Type IXB U-boat *U-106* was built between November 1939 and September 1940 and was subsequently assigned to 2. *Flotille*. Displacing 1,178 tons when submerged and manned by a crew of 58, the vessel's primary weapons were its 22 21-in. torpedoes that could be fired from four bow and two stern tubes. The U-boat also had a SK C/32 105mm naval gun mounted forward of the conning tower, plus quad and single C/38 20mm cannon (in FlaK 30 form) on rear 'bandstands' for protection from aircraft. Three mobile MG 42 7.92mm machine guns could also be fired from the conning tower. *U-106* undertook ten patrols and was credited with the sinking of 22 ships with a total weight of 138,581 gross tons. The vessel was sunk by a Sunderland from No. 461 Sqn off northern Spain on 2 August 1943.

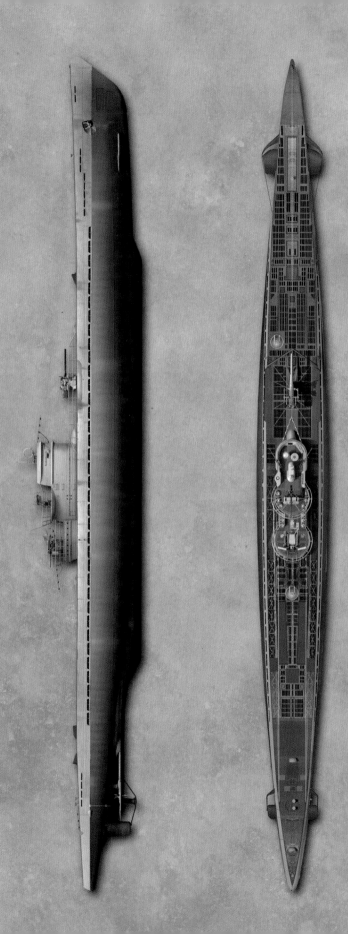

Unrefuelled Type VIIs could barely reach North America's Atlantic Coast. Once there, they had to operate as individual U-boats rather than in more effective wolf packs. These vessels were forced to rely on Type XBs and Type XIVs, which carried fuel, supplies and spare torpedoes to resupply them in-theatre. This in turn made supply U-boats the targets most prized by RAF Coastal Command. As these vessels avoided surface warships, they were the natural prey of ASW aircraft. Most were sunk in attacks from the air.

All of the German U-boats were vastly superior to their World War I counterparts. Type VII and Type IX boats had a test depth of 230m, while the Type X could reach 220m – all three could safely descend deeper than submarines from any other nation. Powered by highly reliable diesel engines and electric motors, they could attain speeds of 17–18 knots on the surface and 7.6 knots submerged. They were armed with 55.3cm torpedoes that boasted warheads three times the weight and four times the power of the 45.5cm (17.7in) weapons carried by World War I U-boats. The improved Type IXs also had a phenomenal range, with the Type IXD almost being able to circumnavigate the globe without refuelling.

Nevertheless, they also had limitations. Both types needed to remain surfaced at least eight hours a day to recharge the batteries that drove the electric motors when the U-boats were submerged. This meant they were designed to primarily operate surfaced. Doctrine called for night-time attacks on convoys while surfaced, allowing crews to use the U-boats' superior surface speed and avoid sonar detection. Although this tactic worked well in the early war years, by 1943 most Allied ASW aircraft and convoy escort ships were equipped with radar capable of detecting surfaced enemy submarines.

U-boats relied on silence to avoid detection. Employing active sonar or radar to locate enemy vessels allowed Allied warships to detect and track a U-boat using them. That limited U-boat crews to visual observation – a five- to 15- mile radius around a surfaced submarine. It also forced them to rely on constant radio communication to coordinate attacks on convoys. By mid-1943, many ASW warships had High-Frequency Direction Finding (HF/DF) equipment to detect and locate broadcasting U-boats, although its effectiveness was eventually negated when the Kurier burst-transmission system was installed in German vessels from mid-1944 onward.

U-39 was one of the original Type IX U-boats built for the Kriegsmarine, being commissioned in 1938 and sunk on 14 September 1939 by two British destroyers just 27 days into its first patrol. The Type IXs, and their variants, were intended as long-range submarines intended to operate individually in convoy-free distant waters. Some 194 were commissioned by the Kriegsmarine between 1938 and 1945. (Getty Images)

U-454

Type VIIC U-boat *U-454* was built between July 1940 and July 1941. Assigned to *7. Flotille*, the vessel participated in ten patrols and sank two ships and damaged a third. *U-454* was sunk in the Bay of Biscay by depth charges dropped from a Sunderland of No. 10 Sqn on 1 August 1943.

Specification

Displacement	769 tons surfaced, 871 tons submerged
Dimensions	67.10m (220ft 2in.) x 6.20m (20ft 4in.) x 9.60m (31ft 6in.) overall, with 50.50m (165ft 8in.) x 4.70m (15ft 5in.) pressure hull
Propulsion	two supercharged Germaniawerft, six-cylinder, four-stroke M6V 40/46 supercharged diesels, rated at 3,200bhp; two AEG GU 460/8-276 electric motors, totalling 750shp (550 kW)
Test depth	230m (750ft)
Speed	32.8 km/h (17.7 knots) surfaced, 14.1 km/h (7.6 knots) submerged
Range	15,700 km (8,500 nautical miles) at 19km/h (ten knots) surfaced, 150km (80 nautical miles) at 7.4km/h (four knots) submerged
Fuel	diesel
Crew	46 officers, petty officers and sailors
Armament (1943)	five torpedo tubes (four bow, one stern) 1453.3cm (21-in.) torpedoes one twin 20mm FlaK 30 anti-aircraft gun one single 20mm FlaK 30 anti-aircraft gun

TECHNICAL SPECIFICATIONS

SUNDERLAND

The Sunderland's impressive structure consisted of an all-metal aluminium fuselage, wings and tailplane, with aluminium sheet metal covering aluminium frames. The control surfaces, ailerons, elevator and rudder used fabric covering over a metal frame. Surfaces were attached to the frames with countersunk rivets, yielding a smooth surface.

The fuselage served as the hull when in the water, the Sunderland being exclusively a flying boat. It had to be placed on beaching gear (a trolley) while in the water before being moved ashore. The hull was constructed of anodised aluminium to resist salt corrosion. The hull form was that of a planing boat, depending on hydrodynamic rather than hydrostatic lift to permit takeoff. It had a broad transverse 'V' shape that came to a knife-edge at the end of the planing surface. A keel ran the length of the hull, and it had a discontinuous 'step' located under the wing. Aft of the step, the hull was shallower. During takeoff, the pilot would 'unstick' the aircraft, rotating forward slightly to lift the aft hull out of the water. This reduced the area in contact with the water, aiding takeoff.

The hull was relatively fragile, which meant the Sunderland required sheltered waters for a safe take-off – waves in excess of four feet in height could shred the hull. The wing-end pontoons were even more delicate, and they could be ripped off in

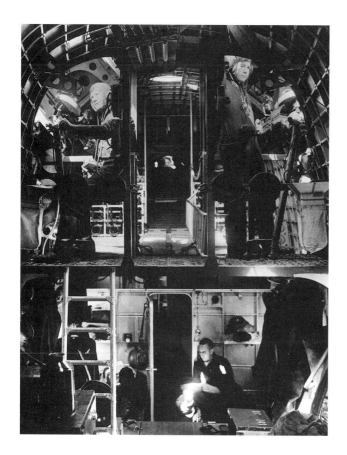

The size of the Sunderland is demonstrated by this photograph of a Mk I. The hatch gunners have each manned their single GO weapons, spare circular magazines for which can be seen secured to the side of them, looking forward from behind the waist gunners' position. Forward of their location is the flightdeck, while on the deck below through the open door is the galley and, beyond that, the wardroom. (Philip Jarrett Collection)

moderate seas. Although landing in open water was inadvisable, it was done on numerous occasions.

The fuselage had a deep, broad cross section, housing two decks forward. The flightdeck contained the pilots' position and workstations for the flight instrument panel, navigator, radar operator and radioman. Originally, the waist gunners were located at the back end of the flightdeck aft of the bomb room, but they were replaced by a powered dorsal turret in the Sunderland II. Below the flightdeck was the forward entry hatch and wardroom, and ahead of the latter was the mooring compartment with the anchor (the bow turret was retractable to facilitate mooring). Aft of the bomb room on the lower level were the galley and bunks. There were hatches on either side of the galley that were used for access when boarding, but which later held machine guns during combat.

The wings were of all-metal cantilever construction. The main spar was made up of two T-beams braced vertically and diagonally by struts, forming a box girder. The engines were faired into the wings with circular monocoque cowlings. Each wing held three self-sealing fuel tanks, one outboard of the outer engine, one between the engines and one between the fuselage and the inner engine. They could carry up to 2,552 Imperial gallons of fuel. Tailplane and fin construction was similar to the wing. They were attached by stub sections on the aft fuselage, simplifying removal and replacement.

The Sunderland's hull was improved during its long production run, with the Mk III featuring a modified design that improved the flying boat's seaworthiness. It also replaced the abrupt step of the previous versions with a faired hull step, thus making take-off easier and reducing drag by ten per cent when aloft. The latter also meant increased endurance.

The prototype and Sunderland I were powered by four 1,010hp Bristol Pegasus XXII nine-cylinder air-cooled radial engines, each driving a three-bladed, two-pitch propeller. One disadvantage with the latter was that it could not be feathered (turned in the direction of flight). If an engine failed, its propeller, driven by the slipstream, continued to turn. This 'windmilling' created drag, further reducing the aircraft's engine-out performance. This meant that although Pegasus XXII-equipped Sunderlands had sufficient power when all four engines worked properly, they became underpowered if one failed. Four engines had been specified by the RAF for the Sunderland I, so that the flying boat could continue to perform its long-range patrol mission even with a Pegasus shut down. However, as the Sunderland grew in weight with the addition of more equipment, it became more underpowered.

The Pegasus XXII was replaced by the 1,065hp Pegasus XVIII as production switched to the Sunderland II in August 1941, the 'new' engine simply being a XXII with the addition of a two-speed turbocharger. It was also designed to use 100-octane aviation fuel, rather than the 85-octane of the earlier engine. Although the extra 220hp ameliorated the power issue for a while, the XVIII still used the same non-featherable propellers as the XXII. Later marks of Sunderland were also subject to the weight gain trends as the Mk I, and began suffering power problems.

The solution was to replace the Pegasus engine with a new and more powerful one. This took the form of the US-designed and built 1,200hp Pratt & Whitney R-1830-90 in the Sunderland V. Known as the Twin Wasp, its 14-cylinders were set in two seven-cylinder rows. Also used by the Hudson and Catalina, the Twin Wasps gave the flying boat a marked improvement in performance – unlike Pegasus-powered Sunderlands, the Mk V could remain airborne with two engines shut down on the same wing.

As designed, the Sunderland was intended to fly missions of up to 13 hours (hence the bunks and galleys), and the Mk Is routinely flew patrols of that duration. The range increased still further with the installation of the Pegasus XVIIIs. One often-unheralded advantage of 100-octane fuel was the ability to lean the mixture when cruising. This meant less fuel was burned per hour, increasing endurance. Aggressive leaning could increase range by as much as a third. While Sunderland crews tended to be more conservative, mission durations increased to 14 hours following the introduction of the Sunderland II and to 16 hours with the Sunderland V. While this was not enough to allow the aircraft to patrol the central Atlantic from the British Isles, the extra loiter time increased the Sunderland's effectiveness over the Bay of Biscay.

The Sunderland's primary weapons when engaging U-boats were bombs and depth charges. In 1939, the RAF had 100lb and 250lb anti-submarine bombs in their inventory for RAF Coastal Command use. Neither had been tested pre-war against U-boats and both soon proved useless against submarines. The 250lb bomb required a direct hit to damage a U-boat, and even then it was unlikely to sink the vessel. However, the weapon had utility against blockade-running merchantmen. Furthermore, aside from the Mk VII depth charge, it was the only minimally effective weapon in RAF Coastal Command's inventory through to January 1941. While Sunderlands carried them until July 1941, and two U-boats were forced to scuttle after they had been targeted by the weapons, not a single German

The Sunderland lacked a traditional bomb-bay. Instead, bombs or depth charges were loaded on to racks which ran out under the wings. The flying boat could carry depth charges or bombs, and in this early-war photograph of Sunderland I N9027 of No. 210 Sqn, the aircraft is armed with almost worthless 250lb anti-submarine bombs. Their main utility lay in convincing U-boat crews to scuttle. (Philip Jarrett Collection)

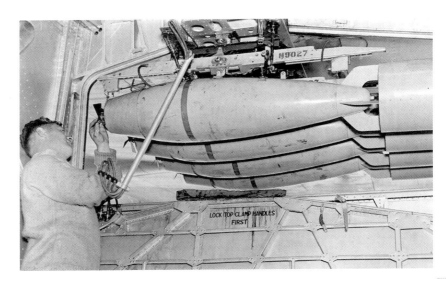

The Sunderland's FN 11 bow turret could be retracted backwards once the flying boat was on the water to provide access to the ground tackle used to moor the aircraft. These crewmen are securing ropes from a buoy to the Sunderland's folding mooring bollard. (Wikimedia)

submarine was sunk by a direct hit from an anti-submarine bomb dropped from the flying boat.

The two main anti-submarine weapons carried by Sunderlands were the Mks VII and VIII airborne depth charges. The former was a modification of the standard Royal Navy Mk VII depth charge. The airborne version had nose and tail fairings that broke off when it struck the water – it had to be dropped at speeds of less than 150 knots and no higher than 150ft above the water. Weighing 450lb, of which 290lb was an explosive charge of TNT, the Mk VII was available in very limited numbers when the war commenced.

The Mk VIII depth charge weighed 246lb, of which 170lb was Torpex explosive. Designed to fit standard 250lb bomb racks, the weapon was developed from January 1940 after the ineffectiveness of the anti-submarine bombs was discovered. Progress was slow, however, and Mk VIIIs did not start reaching operational squadrons until May 1941. Thereafter, it became the Sunderland's 'U-boat killer', especially as the flying boat was incapable of carrying homing torpedoes and was never fitted with anti-submarine rockets. Both depth charges were fused to explode at a depth of 25ft, which was deemed to be optimal for damaging a surfaced or just-diving U-boat.

A. 250lb anti-submarine bomb
The 100lb and 250lb anti-submarine bombs were RAF Coastal Command's primary weapons for attacking U-boats at the start of World War II. The latter bomb is depicted here in artwork. Untested against submarines, the 100lb weapon proved useless against the pressure hull of a U-boat – the latter was able to withstand a direct hit from the bomb. The 250lb bomb was only a little better, being able to damage a U-boat if a direct hit was achieved.

B. 450lb Mk VII air-dropped depth charge
RAF Coastal Command fielded two types of airborne depth charges, with the 450lb Mk VII air-dropped depth charge being the largest. Available pre-war, it was a modified version of the standard Royal Navy Mk VII depth charge used by warships – it had nose and tail fairings that detached when the weapon struck the water. The Mk VII had to be dropped at speeds of less than 150 knots and no higher than 150ft, otherwise the weapon was destroyed upon hitting the water. Weighing 450lb, of which 290lb was an explosive charge of TNT, the Mk VII was set to detonate at a depth of 25ft.

C. 250lb Mk VIII air-dropped depth charge
The Mk VIII depth charge weighed 246lb, of which 170lb was Torpex explosive. Designed to fit standard 250lb bomb racks, the weapon was developed from January 1940 when RAF Coastal Command units complained about the ineffectiveness of their anti-submarine bombs. Almost 18 months passed before the Mk VIII reached operational squadrons, and it proved to be a vital weapon for the Sunderland, in particular, as the flying boat was unable to carry homing torpedoes or rockets. Like the Mk VII, the Mk VIII had to be dropped within strict parameters – a maximum speed of 173 knots and no higher than 750ft – for it to be effective.

D. 250lb Mk VIII air-dropped depth charge
Key

1. Bung	4. Primer tube	7. Suspension lug
2. Mk X pistol and depth adjuster	5. Detonator	8. Sponge rubber pad
3. 170lb of Torpex explosive filling	6. Primer	

SUNDERLAND AIR-DROPPED WEAPONS

A

B

C

LUG

DEPTH CHARGE A/C
250LB MK XI

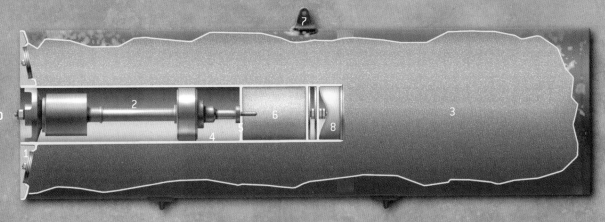

D

Sunderlands also carried 0.303-in. Browning machine guns, these weapons being British license-built versions of the M1919 Browning used by US armed forces and chambered to fire the British 0.303-in. rifle cartridge. With an 11g round and a muzzle-velocity of 2,800ft per second, the 0.303-in. weapon fired 1,150 rounds per minute over a maximum range of 1,000 yards. The Sunderland I originally carried seven 0.303-in. machine guns – one Vickers Gas Operated (GO) weapon (also known as the Vickers K) in a Nash & Thompson FN 11-powered nose turret, two GO guns in hand-held waist positions and four Brownings in the FN 13 tail turret.

Taken in May 1941, this official photograph shows an FN 13 rear turret recently installed in a Sunderland I as it neared completion on the Shorts production line. The FN 13 was replaced by the FN 4A in the Sunderland II, the new turret featuring the same armament of four 0.303-in. machine guns but with twice the ammunition capacity – 1,000 rounds per gun. The rear turret's primary purpose was defence against German aircraft (the main threat to a Sunderland). The rear gunner had two important duties to perform during attacks on U-boats. He suppressed anti-aircraft fire from the U-boat after the attack and was the man best positioned to see the results of any bombs or depth charges that were expended. (Philip Jarrett Collection)

The Sunderland's armament was soon up-gunned to eight machine guns, with twin Brownings installed in the powered turret forward and the FN 13 making way for the FN 4A. Late-production Sunderland IIs replaced the Vickers GOs guns in the waist with a twin-gun FN 7 dorsal turret, but the hand-held weapons soon reappeared as crews installed them in the galley hatches for extra firepower.

The 0.303-in. Browning was out-ranged by the 20mm cannon carried by German long-range fighters hunting Sunderlands over the Bay of Biscay. A 0.303-in. round also proved to be incapable of penetrating the hull of a U-boat, although the machine guns were useful when it came to suppressing a submarine's anti-aircraft fire, as their weapons had no shields to protect the crew. However, the Browning's short range reduced its effectiveness as a strafer. Furthermore, with only two forward-firing guns (in the bow turret), the Sunderland lacked firepower. Crews in Sunderland IIIs eventually added two to four fixed forward-firing 0.303-in. weapons that were operated by the pilots, thus increasing the flying boat's effectiveness as a strafer.

Radar also quickly became one of the Sunderland's key weapons in ASW. Different ASV systems were installed in the aircraft, with the ASV Mk I entering operational service with 25 Sunderland Is from October 1940. Capable of detecting a target at a distance of ten miles, it proved unreliable, required extensive maintenance and was used mainly for navigation rather than U-boat detection. It was replaced by the ASV Mk II from October 1941, with the latter system being the first to enter series production. Using a 1.76m wavelength, it could spot a target up to 36 miles away but had a minimum range of one mile. The latter made its usefulness limited, forcing crews to spot U-boats visually (difficult during the day and almost impossible at night) as the aircraft closed in to attack.

Although the installation of Leigh Lights in other RAF Coastal Command types fitted with ASV Mk II radar solved this problem, the former were never added to the Sunderland, forcing crews to have to rely on flares and luck. Regardless, ASV Mk II

FN 11 BOW TURRET

The Sunderland's bow turret went through three manifestations. The first, proposed by Short Brothers, was a single 37mm autocannon in a powered turret. The RAF vetoed that proposal, opting instead for a single Vickers GO (also known as the Vickers K) 0.303-in. machine gun in a Nash & Thompson FN 11 turret. This gave the Sunderland I seven 0.303-in. machine guns in total. This was judged as too little firepower forward, and the Sunderland II replaced the GO with the twin 0.303-in. machine gun version shown here, which used belt-fed Brownings. This remained the standard nose turret fit on all subsequent Sunderland variants. All bow turrets could be retracted to permit access to tackle for mooring a Sunderland.

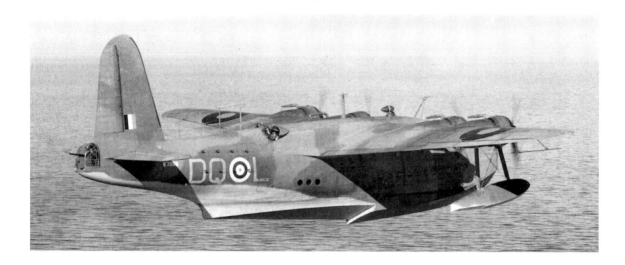

Late-build Sunderland II W3989 of
No. 228 Sqn carries out a patrol
from Oban on 11 July 1942. The
aircraft is fitted with antennae for
ASV Mk II radar system, which had
reached Sunderland units from
October 1941. A long-serving
aircraft, W3989 shuttled back
and forth between Nos. 228 and
202 Sqns before being relegated
to training duties with No. 4
(Coastal) OTU and No. 302 Ferry
Training Unit. It was struck off
charge on 23 February 1945.
(Philip Jarrett Collection)

OPPOSITE
The port waist gunner trains his
Vickers GO 0.303-in. weapon
skyward for the benefit of the
photographer during a flight in
the early months of World War II.
The flying boat's rather
inadequate GO weapons were
replaced in late-production
Sunderlands with a twin-gun FN 7
dorsal turret. The hand-held
Vickers guns were not discarded,
however, with crews installing
them in the galley hatches
directly below the wing roots for
extra firepower. (Philip Jarrett
Collection)

improved the flying boat's effectiveness in the 1942 Bay Campaign until the fielding
of Metox radar detectors by U-boats in August 1942.

In April 1943 ASV Mk III appeared, the radar using microwave frequencies
(approximately 3,300Mhz) invisible to Metox. It could sweep a larger arc than the
Mk II system, and eliminated fade-out at ranges closer than a mile. Although its
introduction eventually led to the slaughter of U-boats, the availability of the Mk III
system was initially limited and Sunderlands ended up getting it late. This in turn
meant that for much of the period when Metox was used, flying boat crews played the
role of 'scarecrow'. They broadcast continuously with their ASV Mk II sets so as to
force U-boats to submerge while crossing the Bay of Biscay. However, the introduction
of ASV Mk III restored the effectiveness of ASV Mk II, for the Kriegsmarine assumed
the new radars were homing in on Metox and ordered its use discontinued, thus
allowing Sunderlands with the older system to again find surfaced U-boats.

The Sunderland was manned by a crew of 11–12 – three pilots, a navigator and
seven or eight other crewmen. The latter rotated between the roles of radioman, flight
engineer, radar operator and air gunner. Two pilots were on duty at all times, and they
rotated between the pilot's seat, the co-pilot's seat and being off duty. The navigator
conducted his duties unassisted, working at his table or taking observations through
the astrodome (fixing his position through sun or star sights). Six crewmen manned
the nose, dorsal and tail turrets, the radio, the flight engineer's station and the radar
set. Except during actual combat, the majority of the crew were off watch.

Four crewmen always served as lookouts – the three gunners in their turrets and
the co-pilot. The bow turret gunner and the co-pilot scanned the seas ahead of the
Sunderland, assisted by binoculars. The dorsal and rear gunner watched astern and to
either side. Positions were rotated every hour. Lookouts searched for U-boats, but also
watched for enemy aircraft. A Sunderland's survival was improved when its crew
spotted attacking German aircraft first. The concentration required when undertaking
a visual search was intense, and could not be maintained for much more than one
hour. Hence the need to relieve the lookouts by rotating crewmen and providing
periods of rest. Off-duty crewmen could either nap in the bunks provided in the crew/
galley area or prepare one of the meals eaten during a typical 13-hour patrol.

The three pilots aboard were the captain, the first pilot and the second pilot. The captain, the most experienced and senior pilot, commanded the flying boat. Early in the war, he had had years of experience before ascending to the role of captain. As the war progressed, however, years of experience were replaced by operational flying hours – typically, a few hundred were required for a pilot to be considered for captain. The first pilot had less experience, and was often thought of as a 'captain in training', acquiring enough experience to become an aircraft commander. The second pilot was frequently someone right out of flying school. He traditionally served as the captain's 'dogsbody'. The three would rotate through being pilot-in-command in order to give the pilots operational flying experience and to allow the captain adequate periods of rest.

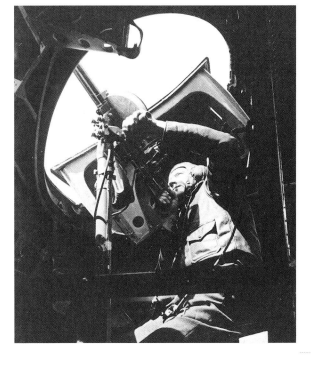

A Sunderland crewman (possibly the navigator) operates the depth-setting control prior to the pilot dropping depth charges. Above him is the FN 11 nose turret, with spare magazines for its 0.303-in. machine gun at top left. The turret appears to be fitted with gun training controls. (Philip Jarrett Collection)

The captain was always an officer, the first pilot generally an officer and the second pilot frequently enlisted. Similarly, the navigator was always commissioned, and frequently the second-most senior man in the crew. The specialist positions – radar operator, radioman and flight engineer – were usually enlisted, typically sergeants, while the air gunners were always enlisted; generally lower ranks, as this was an entry-level position.

During combat, everyone was on-duty. The captain almost always assumed the role of pilot-in-command, even if he had been down for a nap when contact was made. The second pilot took station in the astrodome with the job of observing the battle and providing the captain with regular situation reports. Other off-duty crew would man the guns mounted in the galley hatches, or remain on standby to assist and replace an injured crewman.

U-BOAT

RAF Coastal Command's principal opponents in the Bay of Biscay were Type VII, IX, X and XIV U-boats. The first two were attack submarines, intended to destroy shipping. The Type X and XIV were supply boats that were incapable of attacking ships, but invaluable for extending the operations of the attack boats.

The heart of every U-boat was its pressure hull. Shown here under construction, it was a cylindrical tube capped with hemispheres. The stout framing and heavy plating on the pressure hull allowed a U-boat to resist the ocean's pressure and remain intact at depths of up to 200m. (Author's Collection)

Two Type IA boats (precursors to the Type IX) were sunk in 1940, one with the assistance of a Sunderland, while the Type II U-boat had been withdrawn from the Atlantic in 1940–41. Finally, the Type XXI and XXIII Elektroboots attained operational status too late to be involved in operations in the Bay of Biscay, the Germans having by then lost control of their French ports.

The various Type VIIs built (VIIA, VIIB, VIIC and VIIC/41) represented more than half the U-boat fleet – nearly 700 were commissioned. Type IX variants (IX, IXB, IXC, IXC/40, and IXD) were a distant second, with almost 200 commissioned. Eight Type Xs and ten Type XIVs were built, and they were the most prized targets. Sinking these boats reduced the endurance of the attack boats, especially the short-legged Type VIIs.

Germany had commenced the war with Type VIIA and IX U-boats. The Types' VIIB, VIIC, IXB, IXC and IXC/40 boats that followed were incremental improvements on previous versions, with increased fuel and torpedo storage capacity and marginally better speed. The VIIC/41 was a 1941 improvement of the Type VIIC with a thicker hull, permitting deeper diving.

Which types Sunderlands engaged, especially in the Bay of Biscay, was a matter of chance. The Type VIIs were most commonly encountered due to their numbers and their relatively short endurance, which necessitated more departures and returns from Biscay ports than their longer-legged brethren. A greater percentage of the available Type VIIs were assigned to Biscay ports rather than bases in Norway, as the former offered the shortest distance to the Atlantic shipping routes. Fewer than a quarter of the submarines encountered in the Bay of Biscay were Type IXs, Xs or XIVs.

U-boats all had double-hull designs. An inner hull – a steel cylinder with steel hemispheres at each end – was the pressure hull. Roughly amidships, above the pressure hull, was the conning tower – a cylinder with a hemispherical top. The crew worked and lived within the pressure hull and conning tower, remaining inside when the submarine was submerged. As long as the U-boat stayed within its designed depth parameters, the inner hull maintained a one atmosphere pressure. However, if the water pressure exceeded the ability of the vessel's steel hull to resist it, the hull collapsed, crushing its contents. The exact crush depth was unknown for every U-boat until structural failure occurred – it was below the vessel's test depth, which was the maximum depth an intact U-boat could safely dive to.

The outer casing surrounded the pressure hull, forming a hydrodynamic shell. Although it streamlined the hull, the casing was not designed for optimal underwater movement. It was topped by a flat deck where guns were located, as well as containers for the external stowage of spare torpedoes and other items (including escape rafts). The bridge superstructure rested on the deck, as did platforms for anti-aircraft guns. Fuel and ballast tanks were located on the sides between the two hulls. Ballast tanks could be filled with water or air to allow the U-boat to dive or surface.

The casing and hull combination made a U-boat a difficult object for an aircraft to sink. A hull capable of withstanding water pressure at more than 200m was extremely sturdy, and in order to inflict any proper damage on a submarine it required a direct hit by something capable of cracking the hull open. An air-dropped homing torpedo or a High Velocity Aircraft Rocket (HVAR) could do this. Depth charges, which depended on hydrostatic pressure, had to explode within 15m of a U-boat to do real damage, and that depended on the charge exploding in the water. A direct hit by a depth charge on a surfaced U-boat might fail to open the pressure hull. In some cases, the outer casing absorbed the blast, leaving the pressure hull intact.

Much of the area within the pressure hull was occupied by the two diesel engines and two electric engines (and associated batteries for the latter) that powered every U-boat in service with the Kriegsmarine. All U-boats had two supercharged four-stroke, six- or nine-cylinder diesel engines. These delivered between 1,050 to 2,200hp each. U-boats were also fitted with two electric motors that each generated a total of 750 to 990hp. All of these motors ran off power stored in banks of batteries in the lower half of the pressure hull forward of the engine room.

Diesels are internal combustion engines that produce toxic combustion gases. Running them submerged, without access to the surface to draw air and exhaust burnt fuel, soon asphyxiated the boat's crew. The diesels were run while surfaced, driving both the vessel's twin propellers through geared connections and a generator to charge storage batteries. When the U-boat submerged the diesels shut down, with the electric motors driving the propellers, drawing electricity from the previously-charged batteries.

During the war's early years, when radar and maritime patrol aircraft were scarce, this worked well. Submarines ran surfaced to reach their patrol areas. However, by mid-1942, radar and aircraft made running surfaced hazardous during daylight hours and risky at night. By 1943, daylight surfaced operations were almost suicidal, and even running surfaced at night was hazardous.

In a direct response to this threat, the Kriegsmarine began equipping U-boats with Schnorchels – two tubes (one for air and one for the engine exhaust) – that were raised above the surface of the water when a U-boat was submerged. They allowed the diesels to run, drawing air from the surface. A 'snorting' U-boat using Schnorchels provided a minimal radar and visual profile, with only the tube heads being visible to radar. Nevertheless, snorting was inconvenient, for the U-boat could dive no deeper than periscope depth. If the heads were swamped, the diesels drew air from the submarine until the Schnorchels were again above water.

Twin diesel engines drove a U-boat on the surface and powered the generators that charged the batteries of its electric motors (in this case, two SSW 1 GU 345/34s, with each one capable of generating 990 shaft horsepower) used when submerged. This is one of two MAN M 9 40/46 supercharged nine-cylinder diesel engines used by Type IX U-boats, with each one capable of generating up to 2,200 shaft horsepower. (NHHC)

From 1939 through to the end of 1942, most U-boats only carried a single Rheinmetall 20mm C/30 anti-aircraft weapon, such as this example mounted aft of the conning tower on a Type VIIC vessel. Even after removing the deck gun and supplementing the anti-aircraft cannon, the latter often proved inadequate to fight off an attack from the air. (NHHC)

The U-boat's primary weapons against aerial attack were its Rheinmetall 20mm C/30 or C/38 and 37mm/L83 SK C/30 anti-aircraft guns. When the war commenced, most U-boats were also equipped with an 88mm or 105mm deck gun. The latter weapons, primarily intended for use against merchant ships, were theoretically dual purpose. In practice, deck guns proved useless against aircraft. U-boats rarely found opportunities to use the 88mm or 105mm weapons against surface vessels, and they began to be removed in 1942.

In September 1939, most U-boats carried a single 20mm C/30 or C/38 in an LC 30/37 mount attached to the aft section of the conning tower. When the need for increased anti-aircraft protection became obvious, the single C/30 or C/38 was replaced by a 37mm/L83 SK C/30U or two 20mm cannon in a single mount. Once the deck gun was removed, the weight saved permitted its replacement with multiple 20mm or 37mm guns placed on a 'bandstand' platform immediately forward or aft of the conning tower. The railing on the after platform reminded crews of the metal framework of a greenhouse, resulting in the structure being christened the 'Wintergarten'.

The after platform provided sufficient room for up to three anti-aircraft guns to be mounted. A typical layout can be seen on Type IXC U-boat *U-505*, captured in 1944 and now on display at the Museum of Science and Industry in Chicago, Illinois. It carried two twin 20mm mountings and one single 37mm gun. Many other variants were seen.

The anti-aircraft guns used by U-boats were the 20mm C/30 and C/38 cannon and the 37mm/L83 SK C/30U. Both were designed and manufactured by Rheinmetall. The 20mm weapons were more commonly used than the 37mm cannon, and were fielded in larger numbers. The C/30 and C/38 were similar in performance, both having a 65-calibre barrel (it was 65 times longer than the bore) and firing the same ammunition. The C/30 was older (being introduced in 1930) and heavier (64kg) than the C/38 (57kg), which entered service in 1938. The C/30 had a 20-round magazine. This led to frequent changes of magazine, limiting its practical rate of fire to 120 rounds per minute. The C/38 had a 40-round magazine, which gave it a practical rate of fire of 220 rounds per minute. It was also less prone to jamming than the C/30. A twin-mount variant of the C/38 was developed for U-boats and was capable of being taken to depths of 200m without being damaged.

Both 20mm weapons fired a 0.32kg round, which was 22.8cm long. The projectile weighed between 0.116–0.148kg and was 7.85cm long. Incendiary, tracer and armour-piercing rounds were available. With a bursting charge of 20g, the incendiary round could do significant damage to an aircraft, although typically multiple hits were required to down a Sunderland. Despite the cannon having a ceiling of 3,700m, it was generally ineffective above 1,000m.

U-BOAT ANTI-AIRCRAFT WEAPONS

The C/30 and C/38 20mm and 37mm/L38 SK C/30 were the Flak cannon used by U-boats for anti-aircraft defence. The C/30 20mm and 37mm weapons, both built by Rheinmetall, were contemporaries that entered service in the 1930s. The C/38 20mm was newer, being fitted to U-boats from 1940. It was lighter, had a higher rate of fire and a larger magazine than the C/30 (40 rounds, rather than 20). By 1943 most U-boats were equipped with the C/38, especially using the twin mount (depicted below) designed for the U-boat. The 37mm/L83 SK C/30 (left) was more rarely used, installed in a single LM 42 U mount when fitted to the 'bandstand' of a U-boat.

The primary 37mm gun mounted on U-boats was the Rheinmetall 37mm/L83 SK C/30. Designed in 1930 and entering service in 1934, it was a semi-automatic, single-shot weapon that had an effective rate of fire of 30 rounds per minute. The 37mm/L83 SK C/30 was almost always used in a single LM 42 U mount when installed in a U-boat. The gun weighed 243kg and had an 83-calibre barrel. The 37mm/69 FlaK M42 was a replacement introduced in 1944. It had a 69-calibre barrel and was recoil-loaded from a five-round clip. An automatic weapon, it had an effective rate of fire of 60 rounds per minute. U-boats carried twin or single mount versions of the M42.

The business end of a Flak boat, only four of which were ever fielded by the Kriegsmarine. All of these weapons are C/38 20mm cannon, some in dual mounts and others in quads – Flak boats had single quad mounts forward and aft of the conning tower. (NHHC)

The round fired by the 37mm/69 FlaK M42 weighed 2.1kg, with a 0.742kg projectile that included a propellant charge within each cartridge that weighed 0.365kg. The armour-piercing round carried a 22g Nitropenta bursting charge, while the high-explosive round had a 27.4g charge. The overall length of the projectile was 162mm. It had a ceiling of 6,800m, but as with the 20mm weapon, it was ineffective beyond 1,000m. A well-placed hit (on a wing spar, for example) could bring down a Sunderland with a single shot. This was difficult to do, however, so multiple strikes were usually required to ensure success.

In May 1943, four Type VIIC U-boats – *U-441*, *U-256*, *U-621* and *U-953* – were converted into 'Flak traps' or Flak boats. These vessels had up to four sets of anti-aircraft guns mounted, including quad 20mm and automatic 37mm cannon. Their torpedo load was reduced to a single weapon in each tube and the crew increased in number to accommodate extra gunners. Flak boats were intended to act as surface escorts for U-boats transiting the Bay of Biscay. Doctrine called for them to slug it out with aircraft, submerging only if surface warships appeared. In early May, *Befehlshaber der U-boat* (Commander of the U-boats), Konteradmiral Eberhard Godt, ordered:

Anti-aircraft submarines are to be tried out against enemy aircraft in Biscay. The first of these submarines will leave port at the beginning of May. These boats carry strong anti-aircraft armament and have a lightly armoured bridge and weapons. They are to operate on the surface in Biscay with the specialised task of attacking aircraft.

Initially, the Flak boats proved successful, especially when attacked by single aircraft. On 24 May 1943, *U-441* shot down a No. 228 Sqn Sunderland when it made an attacking run. This proved to be a high-water mark, however, and typical of the encounters with single aircraft. It was a different story when Flak boats were targeted by multiple aircraft, as was the case with *U-621* in May 1943 and January 1944. It was left severely damaged on both occasions after being attacked by Liberators. *U-526* was also attacked by *Liberators* in October and November 1943, although it escaped damage. In all four cases the aircraft involved survived.

Once aware of 'Flak traps', the Allies developed countermeasures that primarily took the form of avoiding single aircraft attacks on U-boats fitted with heavy defensive armament. Instead, the detecting aircraft would call for assistance. After being joined by other aircraft, they all attacked simultaneously from different directions. *U-441* became a victim of one such attack. On 12 July, it fought three Beaufighters and suffered crippling damage.

Discouraged by the lack of downed aircraft and the damage suffered by its small fleet of Flak boats, the Kriegsmarine discontinued the experiment. It abandoned plans to convert three more Type VIIC U-boats – *U-211*, *U-263* and *U-271* – into Flak boats, removing the extra guns and crew accommodation from them and returning the vessels to conventional war patrol duties.

The Kriegsmarine participated in the 'Wizard War', but never as enthusiastically or aggressively as the Allies. Germany adopted radar for U-boats late, and despite knowing the Allies used radio direction finding to locate transmitting submarines, did not install countermeasures in their vessels until late 1944.

Radar detectors, to warn vessels they were being observed, were the first U-boat electronic warfare items developed. The first radar detector deployed was the FuMB 1, better known as Metox, which was introduced in August 1942. A collapsible five-piece wooden frame antenna mounted on the conning tower when the U-boat surfaced, it picked up metre-wave radar emissions. The receiver beeped when radar signals were detected, with the beeping increasing in frequency if the U-boat was detected.

Metox proved effective until April 1943, when the Allies introduced the ASV Mk III centimetre-wave radar system operating on wavelengths undetectable to Metox. Suddenly, the latter was failing to warn of approaching aircraft, which were finding U-boats seemingly without the assistance of ASV Mk II radar – the systems that Metox could detect. Lacking a better explanation, Kriegsmarine scientists suspected the British had found some way to home in on the energised Metox detector. It was, theoretically, possible because the superheterodyne receiver within the Metox equipment emitted a weak signal, allowing its transmissions to be tracked. The Kriegsmarine believed that the Allies were using a high-frequency direction finder to locate U-boats based on their radio transmissions. This meant that 'running down' the direction of the Metox signal allowed an aircraft to precisely locate the emitting U-boat. In practice, however, Metox transmissions were so weak as to be impractical to track, but the Kriegsmarine did not know this.

Amongst those duped was *Iron Coffins* author, Leutnant Herbert Werner, who wrote:

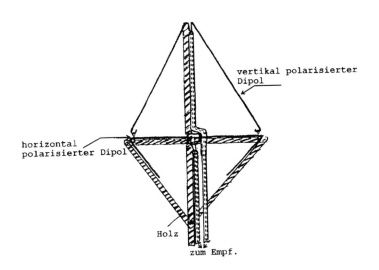

A German wartime diagram of the foldable antenna array for the FuMB 1 radar detector, which was better known as Metox after its French manufacturer. Fitted to U-boats from August 1942, this system warned crews via an audio alert when the antenna detected high frequency radio transmissions from an Allied aircraft's ASV Mk II radar. (Author's Collection)

We were suddenly aware that in our very effort to survive, we had used a device that revealed our position just as clearly as a lighted Christmas tree. For weeks and months, we had been sending out invitations to our own funeral.

In early August 1943 a captured RAF Bomber Command pilot 'let slip' under interrogation that RAF Coastal Command was tracking U-boats by homing in on Metox. This statement was a bald-faced lie, but as it served to confirm the Germans' fears about Metox, they believed him. On 3 August U-boat Headquarters messaged all vessels at sea with the following order:

All U-boats. Attention! All U-boats. Shut off Metox at once. Enemy is capable of intercepting. Keep radio silence until further notice.

The immediate withdrawal of Metox, which in reality was still a highly effective detection system for the ASV Mk II, meant that aircraft (including Sunderlands) still equipped with this earlier radar were now very much back in the hunt for U-boats.

A naval rating examines the antenna for the FuMB 7 Naxos radar detector aboard the Type IXC/40 U-boat *U-889* following its surrender to the Royal Canadian Navy frigates HMCS *Buckingham* and HMCS *Inch Arran* off Newfoundland on 13 May 1945. Unlike Metox, Naxos was permanently fixed and did not have to be disassembled and brought below prior to the U-boat submerging. (Wikimedia)

Once it was realised the problem was being caused by new centimetre-wave radar undetectable by Metox, the Kriegsmarine introduced the FuMB 7 Naxos radar detector, manufactured by Telefunken of Germany. Capable of picking up centimetre-wave transmissions, Naxos was ready for fitment in U-boats from September 1943. Deployment, however, was delayed for three months due to fears the Allies could track U-boats when they activated their Naxos equipment, as had been the case with Metox. By the time it finally entered fleet service, the Allies were introducing search radar systems that were undetectable by Naxos.

From 1944, the Kriegsmarine also began installing passive search radar into U-boats. Both the FuMO 61 Hohentwiel-U and FuMO 63 Hohentwiel-K had a search range of between five and 12 miles – hardly beyond daytime visual range. Although useful for detecting approaching aircraft, neither system lived up to the vastly overestimated range claims made for them by the Kriegsmarine. Most skippers of radar-equipped U-boats misguidedly kept their sets off so as to prevent passive detection, which was not, in fact, actually happening.

Finally, in order to counter the Allies' increasingly effective HF/DF equipment, which was being used to detect and locate broadcasting U-boats, the Kriegsmarine developed the Kurier burst-transmission system. It compressed coded messages from a 20-second transmission time to a 0.25-second burst, which was too short for effective direction-finding. Sea trials were conducted in 1943, but installation lagged and Kurier did not reach operational U-boats until the second half of 1944.

THE STRATEGIC
SITUATION

There should not have been a Battle of the Atlantic in World War II, at least not the one fought throughout the conflict, with U-boats relentlessly stalking merchant ships as they criss-crossed the Atlantic. The tonnage war waged by Großadmiral Karl Dönitz, commanding the Kriegsmarine's U-boat fleet, should have fizzled out by the end of 1940. That it lasted for as long as it did is due to the fact the Allies neglected the lessons in effective ASW they had learned during World War I. Britain began the war unprepared to fight U-boats. By the time the threat they posed had been tamed in 1943, the Third Reich had so much materially invested in the U-boat force it felt it could not simply abandon submarine warfare.

The Royal Navy had eventually negated the U-boat threat in World War I through the adoption of effective convoy tactics and the fielding of ASW aircraft. Once introduced, they combined to tame the Kaiserliche Marine's almost-victorious U-boat offensive in a remarkably short time. In May 1917, with Britain on the verge of starvation, the Royal Navy instituted convoys. Within three months, merchant ship losses had dropped precipitously.

Convoys neutralised the ability of individual submarines to attack using their deck guns. Making a surfaced, gunnery attack on a 30-ship convoy of armed merchantmen was folly. A U-boat had one gun and the convoy 30 to 90. A submerged torpedo attack was possible, but U-boats carried few such weapons in World War I. Finally, convoys slashed the opportunity to find a target. Instead of 30 individually-sailing targets, there was one. The chances of finding a merchantman alone and unprotected dropped by 97 per cent.

The introduction of dedicated ASW aircraft patrols shortly thereafter led to an equally precipitous drop in losses amongst merchant ships. Although the primitive aircraft of the era were unlikely to sink a U-boat, especially when submerged, they nevertheless forced submarines underwater, reducing the crew's field of view to one per cent of what it was when surfaced. Aircraft could also direct warships on to U-boats. The combination of convoys and aircraft all but eliminated the U-boat's effectiveness.

The success of the Allied campaign against the U-boat threat from mid-1917 through to the Armistice defined the world's navies' submarine doctrine between World Wars. All world navies now viewed U-boats as useless as commerce raiders. While submarines increased their effectiveness between 1919 and 1939, the capability of aircraft grew even more dramatically. The fragile wood-and-canvas biplanes of World War I became sturdy, metal-framed monoplanes with significantly more powerful and reliable engines. They had greater speed, greater range and could carry substantially more bombs.

Naval ASW capability had also increased. Immediately after World War I Britain developed ASDIC (SONAR in the US), which tracked submerged objects using sound waves. While imperfect, it made any single submarine's attempt to attack a convoy while submerged a risky proposition. When combined with ASW aircraft and ships sailing in escorted convoys, ASDIC convinced all between-war navies that the submarine's days as an effective commerce raider were over.

Submarines remained in service with navies across the globe, but they were intended for use against other warships. They would also serve as scouts in advance of the battle

Großadmiral Karl Dönitz (shown here addressing U-bootsmänner in Lorient in early 1944) commanded the Kriegsmarine's U-boats and was the architect of the 'tonnage war'. This held that if U-boats could sink merchant ships faster than they could be replaced, Britain would collapse. Germany never achieved that objective, even during 1942 when the U-boat force was at its most effective. (Author's Collection)

line, seeking out enemy vessels. If they found them, with luck, they might pick off a capital ship or two before being sunk by escorting vessels. Exchanging a submarine for a battleship or cruiser was a good trade. Japan and the US went 'all-in', building fleet submarines in considerable numbers. Italy, France and Britain duly followed suit. Germany, however, did not.

Until 1933 it was forbidden from building U-boats. Two years later, construction commenced on new vessels after Germany had signed the 1935 Anglo-German Naval Agreement allowing it to build a U-boat fleet equal in number and tonnage to that of the Royal Navy. Even then, the Kriegsmarine built its boats intending to use them against warships only. Everyone knew U-boats would be ineffective against convoys. Everyone except Kapitän Karl Dönitz, commanding Germany's new U-boat force.

A combat veteran U-boat skipper from World War I, Dönitz believed he could overcome the convoy's advantages. His doctrine called for convoys to be attacked from surfaced U-boats at night. A surfaced submarine was not only invisible to ASDIC, its hull, awash and with only the conning tower visible on a moonless night or opposite

the direction of the moonlight, was virtually invisible to lookouts on escort vessels. Furthermore, the high-sided, looming merchantmen the U-boats were targeting were easily spotted from the conning tower. Such tactics neutralised the strengths of convoys and ASDIC.

Further, Dönitz did not intend for his U-boats to cruise individually. They were to form long search lines to catch convoys as they crossed the Atlantic. The first boat to make contact reported the find to U-boat headquarters ashore, and stalked the convoy. Headquarters then directed the remaining U-boats on to the convoy, which they would attack together. The Germans called this the *Rudeltaktik*. The Allies called it the wolf pack.

Dönitz also came up with the concept of the tonnage war. If his U-boats sank merchant ships faster than they could be replaced, Britain would collapse. Dönitz calculated all he needed was to keep 100 U-boats at sea to achieve this. He started World War II with 57 U-boats, half of which were Type IIs, incapable of patrolling much past the North Sea. Only a third of the remaining 28 could be at sea at any one time. His tonnage war should have been doomed right there.

While Dönitz's tactics mitigated ASDIC and convoys, they did nothing to counter ASW aircraft. U-boats still had to surface to recharge batteries. They had to remain surfaced to shadow or reach convoys. Any nation with a force of adequately equipped ASW aircraft would have been able to thwart attacks on convoys by sinking U-boats cruising to their hunting grounds, or targeting the vessels as they approached a convoy to attack it. Every Admiralty knew that. Britain, however, lacked such ASW aircraft.

RAF Coastal Command was known as the 'Cinderella service' because it was always the last in priority for everything. Its main maritime patrol aircraft, the Anson, was incapable of sinking a U-boat. It could only carry 100lb anti-submarine bombs, which literally bounced off a U-boat's pressure hull. The only other munitions assigned to RAF Coastal Command aircraft in 1939 were 250lb anti-submarine bombs and 450lb air-dropped depth charges. The only land-based aircraft in RAF Coastal Command's inventory at the start of the war that could carry the 250lb bomb was the Hudson, and in September 1939 there was only one squadron equipped with the American twin-engined bomber.

In 1939 RAF Coastal Command was virtually unable to destroy U-boats. The largest weapon its main maritime patrol aircraft, the Anson, could carry was the 100lb anti-submarine bomb, which was incapable of damaging a U-boat even with a direct hit. Here, an Anson I from No. 502 Sqn escorts a convoy off the west coast of Ireland in the summer of 1940. (Tony Holmes Collection)

RAF Coastal Command's most powerful adversary might well have been RAF Bomber Command's leader, Air Chief Marshal Sir Arthur 'Bomber' Harris, who viewed using multi-engined aircraft for anything other than strategic area bombing as a waste of resources. This effectively kept RAF Coastal Command starved of sufficient long-range patrol aircraft until early 1943. (Wikimedia)

A 250lb bomb was unlikely to sink a U-boat in any case – that required a direct hit on a surfaced boat. A near-miss or even a few feet of water between the bomb (which exploded on contact with the water) and the target left a U-boat shaken, but undamaged. The Mk VII 450lb depth charge could sink a U-boat, but Britain was short of them. The shortage hardly mattered, as except for obsolescent biplane flying boats, in September 1939 only nine RAF Coastal Command aircraft could carry this depth charge – the new Sunderlands entering service.

Had RAF Coastal Command been moderately effective in 1939, even one-tenth as effective as it became in 1943, Germany would have run out of U-boats by April 1940. The so-called 'Happy Time' of 1940–41, which saw a high number of Allied merchantmen sunk, would not have occurred, and there would have been no incentive for the Germans to continue with U-boat production. Instead, Britain's inability to counter Dönitz's U-boats led the Germans to massively increase construction. What prevented Britain's defeat in 1940–41 was the simple fact that the Kriegsmarine could not get enough U-boats at sea to win the tonnage war. Nevertheless, U-boats still inflicted a terrible toll on Britain's merchant navy.

By the end of 1941, RAF Coastal Command had started to turn things around. It finally had an effective ASW weapon in the 250lb air-dropped depth charge, which could be carried by all RAF Coastal Command aircraft. A growing number of the latter were also now equipped with ASV radar. The Leigh Light was about to enter service, and weapons like the HVAR and air-dropped homing torpedo were under development. Finally, effective ASW tactics had been developed.

The Kriegsmarine used the grace period it had been given by the Allies in the early-war years to create a massive U-boat fleet. In 1942, there would regularly be 100 or more such vessels at sea on most days of that year. Although U-boat production was accelerating, RAF Coastal Command remained the 'Cinderella Service', starved of aircraft by the insatiable demands of a rapidly expanding RAF Bomber Command, whose leader (from February 1942), Air Chief Marshal Sir Arthur 'Bomber' Harris, was as obsessive about strategic bombing as Dönitz was about the tonnage war. Harris succeeded in seizing almost all RAF aircraft capable of long-range maritime patrol for employment as strategic bombers. Liberators, for example, were excellent maritime patrol aircraft but mediocre area night bombers. Of the first 120 Liberators sent to Britain, RAF Bomber Command expropriated 108, allowing RAF Coastal Command just 12.

Priorities did not change until disaster threatened in 1942. One thing making Sunderlands so valuable to RAF Coastal Command was that they could not be poached for night bombing raids. Not until 1943 did it get a fair allocation of aircraft resources. Unsurprisingly, that proved to be the critical year for the Battle of the Atlantic.

1942 had seen the initiation of the Bay Campaign, with RAF Coastal Command using aircraft to prevent U-boats crossing the Bay of Biscay. The Sunderland squadrons participating in the offensive were a major reason for the Bay Campaign's successful containment of the U-boat threat in 1943.

THE COMBATANTS

The Battle of the Atlantic, particularly the air war fought between RAF Coastal Command and the Kriegsmarine's U-boat forces, pitted two sets of volunteers against each other. Both the RAF and the Kriegsmarine were purely volunteer services of their nations' armed forces. This was doubly true for those actually engaged in combat. After volunteering to join the RAF, aircraftmen had to volunteer for flight duty. Similarly, a Kriegsmarine sailor had to volunteer to serve aboard U-boats. This would remain the case through to 1942.

Both sets of combatants were technically skilled. Most were young, in their late teens or early twenties, although a few of the U-bootsmanner were in their 30s or 40s. Those men were almost all senior enlisted personnel or officers. Amongst RAF Coastal Command aircrew, anyone in their 30s was considered an 'old man'. The demands of flight duty and submarine service required men who were literate, of above-average intelligence and capable of operating complex machinery. They had to be physically fit, have good eyesight (especially aircrew) and be capable of working under pressure. As a direct result of these requirements, this campaign was fought on both sides by the best men their countries could muster.

RAF COASTAL COMMAND AIRCREW

The Sunderland aircrew who fought the U-boats during World War II were members of RAF Coastal Command, which had been established in July 1936 – a year after the Kriegsmarine had formed. The RAF had been created on 1 April 1918, amalgamating the British Army's RFC and the Royal Navy's RNAS. It was the world's first independent air force. Military aircraft of all other nations remained part of their army and navy until the official appearance of Germany's Luftwaffe as an independent air force in 1935.

Flight engineer Sgt Patrick McCombie of No. 10 Sqn enjoys a cigarette – a practice permitted aboard Sunderlands, except when refuelling – whilst resting in one of the four bunks located on the galley deck below the port waist gunner's position. The tubes to the left of the ladder were used for the deployment of parachute flares. (Author's Collection)

To assert independence, the RAF established its own rank structure. What in other air forces were first and second lieutenants became flying and pilot officers, while a captain was a flight lieutenant. Higher ranks gained titles descriptive of their intended commands – squadron leader, wing commander and group captain, respectively, for major, lieutenant colonel and colonel. Oddly, during World War II, except for substituting the term aircraftman for the three lowest ranks, the remaining rank structure mimicked the British Army's – corporal, sergeant, flight sergeant and warrant officer.

Aircraft needed prepared runways to operate, while seaplanes required a sheltered waterway. They also needed fuel and constant maintenance. They had to be hangared. The bigger the aircraft, the longer the take-off run and the bigger the facilities required. Even combat units routinely operated from permanent bases. Personnel slept in bunks and ate in mess halls. Airfields were also typically near towns and cities, and these were routinely frequented by off-duty personnel. During peacetime, RAF service was virtually a nine-to-five job. Despite working with aircraft, the enlisted personnel led lives closer to tradesmen than soldiers or sailors. When not flying, RAF officers led lives closer to that of white-collar workers than the rough living of their army counterparts or the cramped shipboard existence of naval officers. If operating from permanent fixed bases, their lives changed very little during wartime. Even at temporary forward bases, they slept on cots and ate hot meals.

The combination of comfortable conditions and the opportunity to work with (if not fly) aircraft made RAF service popular, even during wartime. The RAF never needed conscription. So many men volunteered, the RAF was able to carefully select recruits in order to maintain high physical fitness and mental acuity standards throughout the war. Even excessive casualty rates failed to dim recruit enthusiasm.

The RAF was a small service compared to the British Army and the Royal Navy. In 1934, it began an expansion in anticipation of a war with Germany. The RAF then consisted of 30,000 regular personnel and 11,000 reservists. When the war started, it consisted of 118,000 regulars and 68,000 reservists. At war's end the RAF's numbers had increased to 963,000. This meant that most RAF personnel, including flightcrew, were not career servicemen. Even those enlisting in peacetime during 1938–39 joined in anticipation of a war. Once the conflict started, those joining the RAF (or the Royal Canadian Air Force (RCAF), Royal Australian Air Force (RAAF) or Royal New Zealand Air Force (RNZAF)) enlisted for the duration of the war.

An RCAF crew from No. 422 Sqn pose on the wing and fuselage of a recently delivered Sunderland III at Oban in the late autumn of 1942. A typical crew during this period numbered 11 to 12 personnel as follows – captain (pilot and aircraft commander), first pilot, second pilot, navigator, flight engineer, radio operator, radar operator and four gunners. Three of these men wear pilot's wings and the rest have observer's brevets, so it would appear that the gunners are missing from the photograph. (Tony Holmes Collection)

In December 1939, the RAF instituted the British Commonwealth Air Training Plan to cope with its massive manpower requirement. A joint military aircrew training programme involving the RAF, RCAF, RAAF, RNZAF and Fleet Air Arm, it coordinated training among all of these air services. Each nation conducted primary training in their own country, although British recruits were sent to Canada for primary flight training. Advanced training was primarily conducted in Canada, although Australia and New Zealand established advanced schools locally later in the war.

All RAF and dominion recruits went through Initial Training, where they learned the fundamentals of RAF service, including military courtesy, 'square bashing' (marching and formations) and weapons training. In Britain, most recruits kitted out at Cardington, in Bedfordshire, before heading to West Kirby, then in Cheshire, for Initial Training. They were then sent to different schools that taught groundcrew specialities and aircrew training. Pilots went through Elementary Flying Training, and if they completed that successfully they moved on to Service Flying Training (equivalent to Advanced Flight Training in the US Army Air Force). Those not selected for pilot training (and those that 'washed out' of elementary flying training) went to one (or more) speciality aircrew schools. These included Air Navigation, Air Observer, Bombing and Gunnery, and Wireless Air Gunnery schools.

Once finished with aircrew training, they were transferred to an Operation Training Unit (OTU). OTUs put the final polish on training. Here, trainees straight out of the speciality schools completed training flying as a crew. The OTUs were organised by aircraft type, with Sunderland aircrew going to No. 4 (Coastal) OTU – the RAF's Flying Boat Training Squadron – at Stranraer, in Scotland, following its formation in March 1941. OTUs bridged the gap between a pure training unit and an operational squadron. On occasion, such as for Operation *Millennium* (the first 'thousand-bomber' raid mounted by RAF Bomber Command, which targeted Cologne) on the night of 30–31 May, 1942, OTUs participated in actual combat missions. Once OTU training was complete, airmen would be sent to an operational unit.

45

The flightdeck of a Sunderland, with the captain keeping his right hand firmly on the throttles while the second pilot signals a nearby convoy with an Aldis lamp. Clearly, this photograph was taken during the winter judging by the fact the captain is wearing a balaclava and the second pilot a greatcoat with its collar turned up. The trio of pilots assigned to a typical Sunderland crew took it in turns to fly the aircraft from the captain's seat. When not at the controls, they would either being resting on the galley deck or scanning for U-boats from the co-pilot's seat. (Author's Collection)

Before World War II, would-be officers attended the RAF College at Cranwell, in Lincolnshire. Opened as a naval aviation training centre during World War I, it became the world's first air academy in 1919. Cranwell was the RAF counterpart to the British Army's Royal Military Academy at Sandhurst, in Berkshire, and the Royal Navy's Royal Naval College at Dartmouth, in Devon. Charged with training the RAF's regular officers between 1919 and 1939, Cranwell cadets were recruited from Britain's public schools (privately-owned institutions that charged attendance fees). Less than one-sixth of its students had attended government or grammar schools. This made the RAF's regular officer cadre an upper class group.

Cranwell closed when World War II started. After that, its officers were drawn from the other ranks. Promising recruits (those with the proper societal background or with extraordinary talent) were commissioned upon completing training. Other ranks' aircrew could also gain commissions over the course of active duty. Promotions were fastest among those with specialist training, especially pilots, observers and navigators. Radio operators, radar operators and even air gunners could gain commissions, albeit in much smaller numbers. Upward mobility tended to be faster in dominion air forces than in the RAF, for those nations were less class conscious than Britain.

In 1936 the RAF was divided into three combat organisations, Bomber Command, Fighter Command and Coastal Command. RAF Bomber Command conducted strategic bombing. As far as those running the RAF were concerned, strategic

HAROLD G. POCKLEY

Harold Graham Pockley was born on 3 February 1913 in Graceville, Queensland, and he grew up in Randwick, a suburb of Sydney, New South Wales. Graduating from Sydney Church of England Grammar School in North Sydney, he worked as a car salesman in Mosman prior to enlisting in the RAAF on 8 January, 1940. Pockley undertook his elementary flying training on Demon biplanes and locally built Wirraways, prior to being commissioned as a pilot officer when he received his wings on 4 May 1940. He went on to complete an advanced course in navigation, attending the RAAF General Reconnaissance School in Laverton, Victoria, and seaplane conversion training at Rathmines, in Lake Macquarie, New South Wales. Promoted to flying officer on 4 November 1940, Pockley departed Australia for England a month later, on 27 December 1940.

His trip to Britain took four months, routing via Canada. Pockley arrived at Mount Batten, a seaplane base on a peninsula in Plymouth Sound, Devon, on 9 March 1941. Here, he was assigned to No. 10 Sqn, the only RAAF unit in Britain then flying Sunderlands, on 9 May 1941. Pockley flew his first operational mission ten days later. After flying as second and first pilot for a year, he was then made captain of a Sunderland crew. The vast majority of his missions during this time saw him operating over the Bay of Biscay — No. 10 Sqn's assigned patrol area.

Pockley was soon dubbed a U-boat 'magnet' by the Australian press, which routinely published reports on the exploits of No. 10 Sqn. On 20 March 1942 — just his third mission as captain — he spotted and sank a German motor launch off Biarritz, France, near the Spanish border. It was the first of many actions he saw that tour. Over the next eight months Pockley and his crew encountered Axis submarines and ships. They attacked at least four U-boats and an Italian submarine, a U-boat supply ship and a blockade-running merchantman. He was credited with sinking two submarines and damaging a third — post-war analysis showed he had only damaged the two credited kills. He also sank an R-boat (minesweeper) and severely damaged two merchantmen, earning him a Distinguished Flying Cross (DFC) and Bar.

As a direct result of his success with No. 10 Sqn, Pockley was frequently featured in stories written by the Australian press. Something of a media celebrity in his home country,

Sqn Ldr Harold G. Pockley in 1944. (Australian War Memorial)

he also acquired a reputation as an expert in ASW. The southeast corner of the Bay of Biscay where he frequently patrolled was dubbed 'Pockley's Corner', more ironically than seriously, by his squadronmates. He returned to Australia in December 1942.

Posted to the RAAF's No. 41 Sqn, equipped with Mariner flying boats, in New Guinea, he became temporary squadron leader on 1 February 1944. Pockley transferred to No. 40 Sqn (also flying Mariners) on 26 September 1944, before being posted home for a rest at year-end when he was given command of No. 7 OTU. He returned to combat in February 1945 when he took command of newly formed No. 200 Flight, equipped with Liberators. The unit was tasked with supporting special forces operations in the Dutch East Indies and Borneo. Pockley was lost while flying No. 200 Flight's very first mission on 25 March 1945, and neither he nor his aircraft were ever found. He was declared dead in November 1946.

bombardment was why the RAF existed. RAF Fighter Command was tasked with air defence. It was seen as the 'glamour arm' of the RAF, with the press at the time depicting its pilots as 'aerial knights' in Spitfires and Hurricanes. RAF Coastal Command was initially responsible for all of Britain's maritime aviation, although in May 1939 the Royal Navy wrested back control of the Fleet Air Arm, which had been part of the RAF since its formation in April 1924. Despite the importance of maritime patrol, RAF Coastal Command was viewed by senior personnel in the RAF as a distraction from strategic bombing. Although its units flew the RAF's longest missions, they were generally equipped with the aircraft the other two commands did not want.

Despite their obsolete equipment and inadequate weaponry, the men assigned to RAF Coastal Command were not the worst the Service had. They could not be, for their missions required competence. They were, however, the most neglected, lacking the glory of the fighter boys or the prestige of the bomber crews. Since the nature of maritime patrol was such that most missions ended without sighting a U-boat, some outside RAF Coastal Command considered such a posting as a non-combat assignment.

Yet their work was hazardous, especially for the crews of the Sunderlands, and doubly so for those patrolling the Bay of Biscay. Combat, when it came, did not involve just U-boats. Flying boats were frequently the target of long-range fighter sweeps by Ju 88s. Like every other Allied aircraft patrolling the area, they were also subject to the hazards of the sea. Crews in Sunderlands did have one key advantage over their brethren in land-based aircraft. They could alight on the water if they found themselves in serious trouble. Such landings were also made when downed aircrew required rescuing, although more than one Sunderland was lost trying to take off again in rough open water after picking up survivors.

Despite the perils facing RAF Coastal Command aircrew, their tours of duty were among the longest in the RAF. Those in RAF Bomber Command flew tours ending after 30 missions or 200 hours in the air, and they were expected to fly no more than two tours. By contrast, a full tour in RAF Coastal Command totalled 800 hours of flying time. That meant an airman assigned to a Sunderland could expect to fly at least 50 and as many as 70 missions before completing a tour and rotating out.

KRIEGSMARINE U-BOOTSMANN

The personnel who manned Germany's U-boats served in the Kriegsmarine, created in May 1935. The latter could trace its lineage back to the Kaiserliche Marine (Imperial German Navy) in 1871. The Kaiserliche Marine became the Reichsmarine in March 1919 following the replacement of the monarchy with a republic. Two years after Hitler took power in 1933, it was renamed the Kriegsmarine, yet it remained essentially the same organisation throughout this time. Senior Kriegsmarine officers began their naval service in the Kaiserliche Marine and were combat veterans of World War I.

When World War II commenced, the Kriegsmarine was an all-volunteer service, and remained so until the conflict ended. Its manpower demands were small compared to the Wehrmacht, which allowed the Kriegsmarine to be picky about those whom it enlisted. High German unemployment pre-war and men preferring naval service to the Wehrmacht during the war years yielded a surplus of applicants – malefactors could be transferred to the army, encouraging good behaviour during the war.

The Kriegsmarine enlisted recruits between 17 and 23 years old. Those under 21 needed parental permission. Applicants had to be physically fit, in good health (including good teeth) and have at least average intelligence. They had to demonstrate that they had completed secondary education and were of German nationality (this included ethnic Germans born in foreign countries). Criminal records prevented enlistment.

Recruits came from all over Germany. Men with prior merchant marine service or appropriate technical skills in mechanics and electricity (including having completed apprenticeships) were preferred. Recruits joined for a minimum of five years. The first year was spent training, with recruits

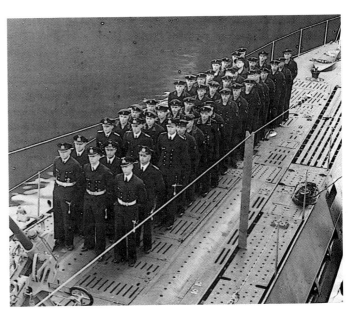

A U-boat crew trained as a team, generally coming together as their vessel was being completed. This is the crew of *U-428*, which had briefly served with the Regia Marina as S 1 before being taken over by the Kriegsmarine on 10 September 1943 following the Italian surrender. The U-bootsmanner were photographed in their best uniforms at Gotenhafen (now Gdynia, in Poland) on 26 October 1943 at the commissioning ceremony for the U-boat. It was typically the last time the crew appeared in formal rig. (NHHC)

being assigned to one of 12 specialities. These ran from being a regular seaman to manning a coastal artillery battery. Half usually became ordinary seamen. Others gained specialised skills needed in the engine rooms, to man the helm, operate weapons or administer paperwork. A few became medical orderlies or musicians.

Basic training for Kriegsmarine recruits was identical to that of Wehrmacht infantry. They wore army uniforms, learned infantry drill and participated in weapons training. After completing basic training, they were sent to specialist schools in Kiel, Mürwick or Swinemünde. Upon graduating from the latter, and having received the rank of matrose (ordinary seaman), recruits were posted to their service assignments. After a year's service, the matrose could expect promotion to matrosengefreiter (able seaman). Long-serving personnel with at least five years' service as a matrosengefreiter could receive promotion to matrosenhauptgefreiter (high able seaman). The rank carried extra respect and prestige, but had no extra responsibility or pay.

An officer's recommendation was necessary for promotion to petty officer (maat), with men accepting promotion lengthening their career obligation to 12 years. Maat candidates went to the *Marineunteroffizierlehrabteilung* (petty officer school) at either Friedrichsort or (after 1938) Wesermünde (in Bremerhaven). There, they were given leadership and combat training identical to army NCOs. They again donned feldgrau uniforms and went through land combat training. During periods of rapid expansion (like in wartime), promising recruits were offered an opportunity to become a maat after basic training. Those accepting promotion went to their specialist training directly after completing basic training, before attending *Marineunteroffizierlehrabteilung*.

A sailor could be promoted to obermate after three years as a maat. Senior enlisted personnel could become warrant officers (the equivalent of senior petty officers in the US Navy and Royal Navy) by choosing one of three career tracks – shore-based, deck and navigation (titles differed for each track). The most senior warrant ranks were given to those considered good enough to be retained after completing their 12-year service obligation.

Kriegsmarine officers came from egalitarian backgrounds, passing through a recruitment process similar to that in place for enlisted personnel. Along with demonstrating a German background, officer candidates also had to provide information on their parents and grandparents to ensure they too were properly German.

Officer training was rigorous. A Kriegsmarine officer was expected to be a competent leader, seaman and navigator. They went through the same basic training as matroses, followed by four months of practical training, depending on their career speciality. Officers followed one of four career paths – they could be line officers (offizier zur see), engineering officers (ingenieur), weapons specialists (waffen-offizier) or administrative staff.

Upon completion of their training, they were promoted to cadet, serving nine months on a training ship. Eighteen months of advanced training followed for line and engineering candidates (two years for gunnery officers), followed by six months of fleet service. Only then were they promoted to leutnant (lieutenant, equivalent to a Royal Navy or US Navy ensign). From then on the promotion sequence was oberleutnant (lieutenant (junior grade)), kapitänleutnant (lieutenant), korvettenkapitän (lieutenant commander), fregattenkapitän (commander) and kapitän (captain). U-boats were generally commanded by an oberleutnant zur see or a kapitänleutnant. More senior U-boat service officers held shore-going assignments.

Enlisted sailors entered the U-boat service only after they had finished their specialised training, and officers joined after completing advanced training. Officers and men serving aboard surface ships (or ashore), however, went directly to active service assignments. Those volunteering for (or being transferred to) submarine duty attended a school to prepare for service in U-boats, initially at the Kiel-based *Unterseebootsabwehrschule* – U-boat fighting school. The name was intentionally ambiguous to conceal that it was not a school dedicated to fighting submarines, but rather how to fight with them.

Officers destined for U-boat service went through a 12-week training course which alternated classroom training with seagoing exercises. This included making 15 successful attacks from training simulators. Upon completion, they then undertook advanced training at sea, which covered boat handling, basic tactical theory and torpedo firing. By 1938 the Kriegsmarine had a flotilla of U-boats used exclusively for

The same crew as seen on the previous page after completing an extended spell at sea in 1942–43. All are scruffy, and many have beards, after a number of weeks at sea. They are also exhilarated at returning to port following a successful patrol. *U-428* served primarily with 23. *Flotille* as a training U-boat, and therefore failed to sink any enemy ships. (NHHC)

such training. These were stationed at Neustadt, in Holstein. During World War II, the training bases were expanded and all tuition was conducted in the Baltic.

Pre-war crews spent up to six months on training boats before being assigned to an operational vessel. Even after the war started, an early lack of available operational boats allowed the Kriegsmarine to maintain a leisurely training schedule as there was no pressing demand for crews.

The crew of *U-96* have assembled on the stern of the vessel to be addressed by Korvettenkapitän Herbert Sohler, commander of *7. Flotille* (to which the U-boat was assigned) prior to leaving Lorient on their second patrol on 9 January 1941. The U-boat's commander, Kapitänleutnant Heinrich Lehmann-Willenbrock (white cap) is standing to attention to the right of Sohler. (Getty Images)

However, by 1942, the U-boat force had rapidly expanded in size to the point where training schedules had to be shortened in order to provide sufficient personnel to man the newly-built vessels. Much of the instruction previously done in training flotillas was now undertaken during the working up of new U-boats.

When a U-boat neared completion, a crew was assembled for the vessel. Prior to launch, the captain and senior crewman assigned to the U-boat were sent to the shipyard. There, they familiarised themselves with the submarine and supervised its completion. In the final pre-launch weeks they were joined by the rest of the crew – typically a mixture of veteran U-boat men and newly trained personnel. After the vessel's launch and completion, the crew conducted three weeks of acceptance testing. This included diving trials, silent running tests and a general shakedown of the U-boat's equipment and machinery.

Combat training followed – a rigorous set of exercises to prepare the U-boat for active service. Deep dive tests and realistic combat exercises were undertaken, with combat veterans accompanying the crew during these exercises in order to declare unexpected equipment 'failures' to test the captain's reaction. This intensive training sometimes had deadly results, and no fewer than 30 U-boats were lost during such exercises.

Initially, the U-boat force was all-volunteer, making it an elite organisation in the war's early years. The explosive expansion of U-boat service changed this, and by 1942 men were being assigned without having first volunteered for submarines. Since the Kriegsmarine was an all-volunteer service, this had less impact on morale and competence than was commonly thought at the time. The U-boat force started out with high morale, and managed to maintain it throughout the war. Crews were still professionals, and the large majority were patriotic Germans.

In a U-boat more than any other warship, individual survival depended on the competence of every crewman. If a submarine was sunk, typically everyone aboard died. A U-boat could sink as easily through mishandling machinery as through combat. Survival motivated high performance. *U-bootsmanner* continued to take the fight to the Allies through to war's end, even when they knew the odds were heavily stacked against them.

WOLF-DIETRICH DAMEROW

Wolf-Dietrich Damerow was born on 28 May 1919 in Schwedt, an agrarian town on the Oder River in Brandenburg. Growing up in the chaos and general poverty of Germany in the 1920s, he was typical of the officers commanding U-boats in 1943–44. Damerow enlisted in the Kriegsmarine on 9 October 1937, attending the *Marineschule Mürwik* (Mürwik Naval School) as part of Crew 37B – the number indicated the year the class of cadets started and the letter the term in which he started. After a year as an offiziersanwärter (officer cadet), he was promoted to seekadett (sea cadet) on 28 June 1938.

A fähnrich zur see (midshipman) from 1 April 1939, Damerow completed a two-year land-based programme on 1 March 1940 and was then promoted to oberfähnrich zur see (senior midshipman) – a rank he kept for just two months. In peacetime he would normally have spent a year at each rank, but the period between promotions was compressed once war began. Damerow was commissioned as a leutnant zur see (ensign) on 1 May 1940, whereupon he became a line officer. His first sea duties were in the surface navy, Damerow serving as a watch officer aboard Vorpostenboots (small warships, usually converted from seagoing fishing boats). They were typically under 1,000 tons in displacement and conducted a variety of minesweeping, ASW, anti-aircraft and patrol duties similar to those performed by Royal Navy armed trawlers. Damerow earned a mine warfare badge during his tenure.

In September 1941 he transferred to the U-boat service, completing training in March 1942. Damerow was then assigned to the newly-launched *U-521* (a Type IXC boat) as part of its Baubelehrung (U-boat construction familiarisation) team; the crew that oversaw the completion of the vessel. When *U-521* was commissioned on 3 June 1942, Damerow became the First Watch Officer (IWO), the submarine's executive officer, serving under its skipper, Kapitänleutnant Klaus Heinrich Bargsten. He participated in *U-521*'s first two war patrols as IWO, the U-boat spending 147 days at sea. The vessel patrolled the North American coast on its first deployment and the Central Atlantic off Spain and Africa on the second. *U-521* was credited with sinking three merchantmen and a Royal Navy corvette for a total of just over 20,000 tons while Damerow was aboard.

Oberleutnant zur See Wolf-Dietrich Damerow. (Author's Collection)

In March 1943, Damerow was selected for the U-boat commander course, and detached from *U-521* (which was sunk off the Virginia coast on 2 June 1943). Damerow completed the course that same month and was given command of the Type IXB vessel *U-106* on 20 June 1943. A veteran boat, *U-106* had completed nine war patrols and sunk 22 ships for a total tonnage of 138,581 tons prior to Damerow taking command.

U-106 departed Lorient on 28 July 1943 in company with *U-107*. Five days out, while crossing the Bay of Biscay, it was caught by two RAF Coastal Command Wellingtons and badly damaged. Later that day, attempting to return to port, the U-boat was attacked by two Sunderlands and sunk. Damerow, on the bridge at the time, was badly wounded. He and 35 other crewmen were rescued by E-boats and returned to a French port. Damerow failed to recover from his wounds, passing away in a military hospital at Eberswalde, in Brandenburg, on 21 May, 1944.

COMBAT

EARLY YEARS

When World War II started, RAF Coastal Command had just three units equipped with Sunderland Is – No. 204 Sqn at Mount Batten, in Devon, and Nos. 210 and 228 Sqns at Pembroke Dock, in Wales. All were assigned to No. 15 Group, whose area of responsibility included the Atlantic Ocean west and south of the British Isles. Crucially, the Bay of Biscay was part of the group's assigned patrol area, although in September 1939 this was a backwater for U-boats. However, following the fall of France in June 1940, this body of water became their 'main highway' to and from the Atlantic through to the summer of 1944. Sunderlands and U-boats would clash over the Atlantic for the next five-and-a-half years, with this duel commencing where it was waged fiercest – over the Bay of Biscay, and the waters surrounding it.

When the war started the Sunderland was almost the only RAF Coastal Command or Fleet Air Arm aircraft capable of sinking a U-boat at sea. It, along with the London and Stranraer biplane flying boats, were the only ASW types that could carry the 450lb Mk VII depth charge. On 3 September 1939, the three Sunderland squadrons could muster 18 aircraft between them. RAF Coastal Command soon added another squadron to its ranks, with nine additional aircraft. On 1 July 1939, the RAAF activated No. 10 Sqn at Point Cook, in Victoria, and it soon became Australia's first Sunderland unit. Seven crews from No. 10 Sqn arrived at Southampton, in Hampshire, later that month to accept delivery of their aircraft from Shorts. They then spent July and August familiarising themselves with the Sunderland, before taking delivery of factory-fresh aircraft in early September.

The RAAF had intended to have its crews ferry the aircraft to Australia, where they would patrol the Pacific and Indian Oceans. The nation's declaration of war against

Germany scrapped that plan. On 20 October, the Australian government committed the squadron to the defence of Britain, and it remained there throughout the conflict.

No. 10 Sqn flew its first operational mission on 10 October 1939. While primarily operating out of Mount Batten, guarding the Southwest Approaches to Britain, including the Bay of Biscay, No. 10 Sqn detachments were sent as far north as Oban, in Scotland, and as far south as Malta and Gibraltar during the course of the war. Along with No. 228 Sqn, No. 10 Sqn patrolled the Bay of Biscay longer than any other Sunderland-equipped unit.

At first such missions were largely uneventful, for U-boats rarely encountered Sunderlands in the war's opening months. There were too few of either, and a surplus of ocean for the U-boats and Sunderlands to play 'hide-and-seek' in. There were only 30 U-boats at sea in September 1939, and this number had halved by year-end. There were generally no more than 24 Sunderlands available to mount patrols at any one time during the same period. The flying boat crews had more than a million square miles of ocean to search, and the U-boats were eager to stay hidden. When they spotted an aircraft they dived. Thus, it is unsurprising that the first encounter between a Sunderland and a U-boat was at one remove – the rescue of the crew of SS *Kensington Court*.

At 1238 hrs on 18 September 1939, the steamer SS *Kensington Court*, carrying a cargo of cereals from Rosario, in Argentina, to Liverpool, was spotted by *U-32* 120 miles west of Land's End. The U-boat surfaced and, in accordance with prize rules, stopped *Kensington Court*, determined it was carrying legitimate military cargo (foodstuff) and saw the 35-man crew off the vessel. At 1400 hrs, *U-32* torpedoed SS *Kensington Court*.

The radioman aboard the merchantman signalled a submarine contact report when *U-32* first surfaced. The transmission drew the attention of a No. 228 Sqn Sunderland flown by Flt Lt Thurston Smith and seconded by Plt Off D. R. S. Bevan-John. By the time the flying boat arrived *U-32* was gone and *Kensington Court*'s crew crowded into a single lifeboat. Bevan-John recalled what happened next:

> Having searched for the sub without success, we decided to try a landing. The sea seemed like a millpond. Flt Lt Smith made an excellent landing on what turned out to be quite a swell. Another Sunderland [from No. 204 Sqn], captained by Flt Lt Jackie Barrett, appeared overhead. He asked if we wished him to land. We replied it was a risky business. He did.

The two Sunderlands collected the crew, 20 in Smith's aircraft and 14 in Barrett's. A third No. 228 Sqn flying boat, commanded by Australian Sqn Ldr Guy Menzies, remained airborne, providing cover against the U-boat's return. They then took-off, which Bevan-John reported 'was somewhat hairy'. The seas, combined with one Sunderland having landed with its bombs on the racks, made for a hazardous take-off. Both aircraft returned safely to Pembroke Dock with their cargo of castaways.

The incident created a sensation, attracting significant press coverage and earning both Smith and Barrett DFCs. It also raised the expectation that if Sunderlands spotted survivors at sea, they would land and rescue them. An open-ocean landing was one of the most hazardous things a Sunderland crew could attempt. The sea always

seemed smoother when flying above it than once on its surface. Several Sunderlands destroyed themselves trying to land or take-off in the ocean, or, finding the seas too rough for a safe take-off, had to taxi to safety.

While the SS *Kensington Court* rescue received widespread publicity, U-boat sinkings by RAF Coastal Command received almost no coverage. During the first two years of the war, if pressed, it claimed this was due to operational security – a reluctance to give the Kriegsmarine information that would allow U-boats to escape from marauding RAF Coastal Command hunters. The real reason was there were so few U-boats believed sunk by aircraft as to be embarrassing. Between September 1939 and the entry of the United States into the war in December 1941, RAF Coastal Command and Fleet Air Arm aircraft sank or captured a total of seven U-boats. The Type IXB vessel *U-64* had been bombed by a Swordfish floatplane operating from the battleship HMS *Warspite* while surfaced and stationary off Bjervik, in Norway, in April 1940. Aside from two more successes later in 1940, the remaining four U-boats had been sunk in the second half of 1941.

Sunderlands assisted in sinking two U-boats in 1940. On 30 January, the Type VIIB vessel *U-55* attacked convoy OA 80G in the Celtic Sea southwest of the Isles of Scilly, sinking the 5,026-ton British motor tanker *Vaclite* and the 5,085-ton Greek-flagged steamship *Keramiai*. HMS *Fowey*, a sloop escorting the convoy, got an asdic contact on *U-55*, pursued it and depth-charged the U-boat. The attack damaged the vessel, causing flooding, but it failed to bring the submarine to the surface. *Fowey* called for help, and the destroyers HMS *Whitshed* and HMS *Ardent*, the French destroyer *Valmy* and the No. 228 Sunderland I captained by Flt Lt Edward J. Brooks duly responded.

Whitshed quickly achieved a sonar contact and launched a second attack against *U-55*. The exploding depth charges further increased the flooding to the point where the U-boat's skipper, Kapitänleutnant Werner Heidel, ordered it to the surface. He had hoped to slip away in low-hanging fog, but the Sunderland crew spotted *U-55* and attacked. The flying boat was armed with inadequate anti-submarine bombs, rather than depth charges, so it was unable to sink the U-boat. Brooks attacked anyway, dropping bombs and strafing *U-55*, while directing surface escorts in the direction of the submarine. *Fowey* and *Valmy* soon spotted *U-55* and opened fire. Unable to submerge, Heidel ordered *U-55* scuttled, and he went down with the

A No. 228 Sqn Sunderland prepares to alight 120 miles west of Land's End on 18 September 1939 in order to rescue the crew of the torpedoed and sinking merchantman SS *Kensington Court*. This rescue (which also involved a Sunderland from No. 204 Sqn), conducted barely two weeks after the war had started, made the flying boat's reputation and encouraged amongst RAF Coastal Command crews the unwise practice of landing on open ocean. (Author's Collection)

55

U-boat – the remaining 41 crew were captured. Although *Fowey* had actually inflicted telling damage on the vessel, the Sunderland crew were awarded shared credit for the kill; an RAF Coastal Command first.

Almost exactly five months later, on 1 July 1940, a Sunderland from No. 10 Sqn was involved in the sinking of *U-26*, one of only two Type IA U-boats in the Kriegsmarine. The vessel was cruising the Celtic Sea southwest of Ireland on the evening of 30 June when its crew intercepted convoy OA 175. After reporting contact, *U-26* conducted a night attack on the convoy. At 0118 hrs on 1 July it torpedoed SS *Zarian*, a 4,871-ton merchantman. *U-26* was then spotted by convoy escort *HMS Gladiolus*, and the corvette left the merchantmen to hunt the U-boat. *Gladiolus* forced *U-26* to dive, whereupon it made sonar contact with the submarine and completed five depth charge attacks.

The first caused severe damage, and by the end of the fifth attack *U-26* was leaking oil and unable to remain submerged. At roughly 0730 hrs it broke the surface just 800 yards from *Gladiolus*. However, the corvette's crew failed to spot the U-boat in the dawn twilight, and its skipper, Kapitänleutnant Heinz Scheringer, managed to guide the vessel away using its electric motors in order to minimise noise.

At 0815 hrs, the No. 10 Sqn Sunderland (again armed with 250lb anti-submarine bombs) captained by Flt Lt Bill 'Hoot' Gibson spotted *U-26* sneaking away. The aircraft guided the sloop HMS *Rochester* to the scene, and spotting the pursuing Sunderland and warship, Scheringer took *U-26* under. Gibson aimed his Sunderland at the swirl of water left by the U-boat and dropped four 250lb bombs. Although the

U-26 was one of just two Type IA U-boats in the Kriegsmarine's inventory at the start of the war. It was attacked twice on 1 July 1940 by the No. 10 Sqn Sunderland captained by Flt Lt Bill 'Hoot' Gibson. The presence of Royal Navy warships nearby, previous damage done by depth charge attacks from HMS *Gladiolus* and the first bombing run by Gibson convinced the U-boat's skipper, Kapitänleutnant Heinz Scheringer, to scuttle *U-26*. (Wikimedia)

1. Flap indicator lamp
2. Switch for flap indicator meter
3. Flap indicator meter lamp
4. Flap angle gauge
5. Flap control switch
6. Switches for air-to-air recognition lamps
7. Ignition switches
8. Clock
9. Drogue signals switchbox
10. Engine revolution gauges
11. Engine boost level gauges
12. Fore and aft attitude gauges
13. Airspeed indicator gauge
14. Altimeter
15. Turn-and-bank indicator
16. Second pilot's bomb release switch
17. Stowage bag for second pilot's firing switch and lead
18. Type P8 compass (early aircraft only)
19. Propeller speed control levers
20. Mixture levers
21. Windscreen de-icing hand-pump
22. Throttle levers
23. Control switch for landing lamps
24. Dipper lever for landing lamps
25. Engine starter pushbuttons (under spring-loaded cover)
26. Morsing switchbox for downward identification lamps
27. Captain's instrument flying panel
28. Distance-reading compass repeater
29. Cockpit lighting
30. Compass correction cards
31. Rudder pedals
32. Card holder (signals)
33. Switch for pitot head heater
34. Captain's press switch for radio
35. Automatic controls main switch
36. Bomb container jettison switch
37. Intercommunication call lamp and push-button
38. Downward identification lamp switch
39. Head or steaming lamp switch
40. Navigation lamp switch
41. Flare-launching button
42. Type P4A compass
43. Bomb selector switches
44. Automatic controls panel
45. Control yokes
46. Captain's seat
47. Second pilot's seat
48. Elevator trim tab control levers
49. Engine master fuel cocks levers
50. Slow-running engine cut-out control levers
51. Fuel jettison controls
52. Rudder trim tab control handle

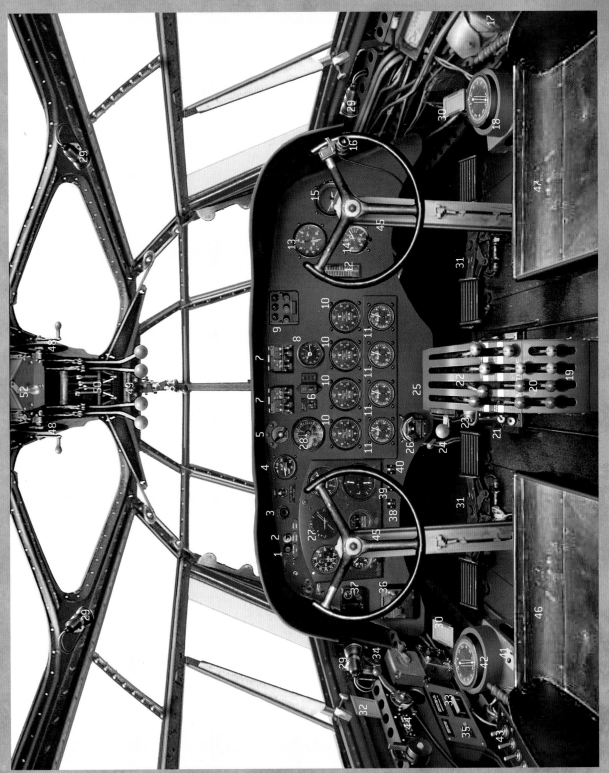

ordnance exploded upon hitting the water, doing no real damage to *U-26*, their detonation convinced Scheringer to resurface and scuttle. The U-boat's *U*-batteries were almost dead, and it was shipping water from *Gladiolus*'s attack.

As *U-26* broached water, Gibson took his Sunderland in for another attack, dropping four more 250lb bombs, which landed off the port side of the U-boat. Again, they did little damage, but *U-26*'s engineering officer had by then opened the scuttling valves and the submarine was sinking. Its crew of 48 all managed to escape and were picked up by *Rochester*. Gibson and his crew were credited with the kill, and his first attack had indeed convinced Scheringer to scuttle. Had it not happened, U-26 might have escaped.

The sinking of *U-26* would be the last confirmed U-boat kill or assist credited to a Sunderland until May 1943. No. 10 Sqn sank another submarine during the intervening period, however. On 10 September 1941, the aircraft captained by Flt Lt Athol Wearne was conducting a sweep of the Bay of Biscay when, seven hours into the patrol some 400 miles west of Bordeaux, its crew spotted a surfaced submarine only 1,000 yards away. The aircraft and U-boat spotted each other simultaneously, and as Wearne turned to attack, the vessel dived. By the time Wearne reached the U-boat it was underwater, but he could see the hull immediately below the surface.

By September 1941 the 250lb Mk VIII depth charge had been in service for four months. Wearne's Sunderland was carrying them, not anti-submarine bombs, and he dropped a salvo on the surface wake. Two made direct hits, resulting in an increasing pool of reddish-brown water appearing 100 yards from where the depth charges had exploded. Three minutes later, the crew of the circling Sunderland saw an oil slick, and when they returned to Pembroke Dock they claimed the U-boat as a kill.

Wearne's crew reported seeing '77' painted on the side of the conning tower, so they assumed they had sunk *U-77*. Admiralty Intelligence soon discovered *U-77* was still afloat – it would survive until March 1943, when an encounter with a Hudson sent it to the bottom. The No. 10 Sqn kill was disallowed, and Wearne was credited with having damaged *U-77*. He and his crew had in fact sunk the Marconi-class Italian submarine *Alessandro Malaspina*, part of a squadron from the Regia Marina operating out of Bordeaux in 1941. The vessel had sailed from Bordeaux on 7 September and was never heard from again. Researchers only discovered the true identity of Wearne's victim in 2004.

CRISIS YEAR

1942 saw more encounters between aircraft, including Sunderlands, and U-boats. While there were still a few Axis blockade runners and patrol craft for RAF Coastal Command to chase down, the primary focus of its patrol squadrons was increasingly on submarines. Although RAF Coastal Command aircraft finally had effective sub-killing weapons by 1942, there were no fatal encounters between U-boats and Sunderlands that year for several reasons.

Sunderlands were rarely patrolling where the U-boats were fighting, with the flying boat's range preventing it from reaching the central portions of the Atlantic where the U-boats were attacking convoys. Additionally, in the first half of 1942, North America's eastern seaboard, far from any Sunderland squadron, was the U-boats' main hunting ground. It was largely undefended, an area where targets were plentiful and escorts, including aircraft, were virtually non-existent.

The Sunderland's primary patrol area remained the Bay of Biscay or waters within eight flying hours of Britain, Iceland, Gibraltar and West Africa. Except for the Bay of Biscay, U-boats avoided those areas. And even when they were in the Bay of Biscay, the vessels were transiting rather than patrolling. In 1942 that meant crossing surfaced at a high cruising speed. Having made it to the open water of the Atlantic Ocean, U-boats then attempted to sink ships. That meant they spent less than a week in the Bay of Biscay during a patrol that might range from 30 to 120 days in duration. By January 1942, only one Sunderland unit (No. 10 Sqn) remained assigned to No. 19 Group, which was now responsible for aircraft patrolling the waters south and southwest of Britain, including the Bay of Biscay. The rest were operating elsewhere, where encounters with U-boats were even less likely.

A 12-strong Sunderland crew squeeze into motor transport for the short ride down to a nearby slipway, where they would board a small tender and be taken out to their flying boat firmly moored to a buoy. All personnel are wearing 'Mae Wests' and flying boots – standard rig for Sunderland crews. (Author's Collection)

Most Sunderland patrols between 1940 and 1942 were typical of the one described in a column written by American war correspondent Virginia Cowles, who joined a No. 10 Sqn crew for a completely uneventful patrol in late 1940:

We left at six o'clock in the morning and flew at a speed of about 150mph. Soon, we were far out at sea with nothing but a solid blue stretch above and below and the sun sparkling on the waves. We hadn't been in the air long before the wireless operator intercepted a message from a flying boat which had been sent out to pick up the survivors of a torpedoed ship, reporting two enemy aircraft. A few minutes later we picked up a second message – 'enemy out of sight'. During the next four hours the only object we saw was one small trawler, a Spanish fishing boat.

Shortly after lunch I thought we were going to have some excitement when the flying boat suddenly swung off course. Far below, there was a long patch of oil on the water. He [the pilot] muttered 'submarine' and scrambled up the ladder to the cockpit. Suddenly, it was all over. The all-clear sounded, the boat gained altitude and straightened out. 'Just some old wreckage'.

There were no further incidents that afternoon, and we patrolled hour after hour with only sea and sky stretching endlessly before us. We landed in the harbour just as it was getting dark.

For Cowles it was a glorious adventure, yet this uneventful trip from tedium to ennui was the daily reality for Sunderland crews patrolling the Bay of Biscay.

Sometimes there were encounters. One occurred on 5 June 1942, involving the Type VIIC U-boat *U-71*, which had left La Pallice the previous day. It was at the start

On its fifth war patrol, from 23 February through to 20 April 1942, *U-71* sank five ships for a total of 38,894 tons. That included the 8,046-ton American tanker SS *Dixie Arrow* shown here ablaze and sinking off the North Carolina coast on 26 March after being torpedoed. (National Archives)

of its sixth war patrol, all of which had been under the command of Kapitänleutnant Walter Flachsenberg. In a hurry to reach his patrol assignment, Flachsenberg decided to run surfaced for the first 24 hours at sea. He felt the odds of encountering an enemy aircraft close to the French coast were low, and good lookouts would warn him of any approaching aircraft in time to dive safely. It was a clear, cloudless day, and visibility was good.

Flachsenberg had been attacked by aircraft once before. On 30 November 1941 he had been taking *U-71* to the Mediterranean when he was targeted by a Whitley. With *U-71* having escaped unharmed that time, perhaps Flachsenberg believed other air attacks would be similarly benign.

At 1325 hrs on 5 June the No. 10 Sqn Sunderland captained by Flt Lt Sam Wood reached its patrol area. Flying at 5,000ft, the crew were monitoring an area 200 miles west of the U-boat pens at La Pallice. At 1545 hrs, the radar operator reported a contact eight miles from the Sunderland's starboard bow. Wood turned towards the contact and soon spotted a submarine fully surfaced dead ahead. He immediately dived to attack.

Good fortune had placed the sun directly behind the Sunderland as it approached *U-71*, whose inexperienced lookouts failed to spot the flying boat until it had closed on them. Flachsenberg ordered an immediate dive, and by the time Wood's Sunderland reached the release point *U-71* was underwater. Undeterred, Wood dropped eight Mk VIII depth charges 130 yards ahead of where swirling water indicated the U-boat had gone under. A minute after the depth charges exploded, *U-71* surfaced. The Mk VIIIs had ruptured *U-71*'s aft buoyancy tanks, and the U-boat began heading to the sea bottom. Flachsenberg ordered all ballast tanks blown, stopping the dive just before *U-71* reached crush depth. After that, an uncontrollable rise took *U-71* up until it broke water at a 40-degree-up angle. *U-71* smacked down motionless on the water, listing 15 degrees to port. The crew were temporarily dazed, diesel oil leaked out of the hull and a big air bubble appeared alongside the conning tower.

While significant, the damage was not fatal, and Wood was out of depth charges. As *U-71* lay motionless on the water, the Sunderland made repeated passes over it. The gunners on board the flying boat began to hose down *U-71* with 0.303-in. machine gun fire, emptying 2,000 rounds into the vessel. The bullets were too light to do significant damage, however. Finally, Flachsenberg and the gun crew exited the conning tower and the latter manned the 20mm cannon, returning fire at the Sunderland. After receiving a few hits, Wood realised that while he was unable to damage *U-71*, it could shoot him down. He withdrew to just beyond the range of the 20mm battery, flying around the submarine as the radio operator tapped out a contact report, requesting fresh aircraft be sent. None were available.

As the flying boat circled, the crew of *U-71* made repairs. Within two hours it was underway again, smoke and steam boiling out of the engine room vents. Flachsenberg performed a few 'figure-8s' to test his steering before finally bringing *U-71* up to a speed of eight knots and submerging, disappearing from view of the frustrated Sunderland crew flying impotently over it. The U-boat headed back to La Pallice to be repaired and Wood returned home.

By the time this action took place a new Australian Sunderland unit, No. 461 Sqn, had been activated at Mount Batten in late April 1942 and also assigned to No. 19 Group. Attacks such as those on *U-71* convinced the Germans the Allies had airborne radar. To them it must have seemed like it only worked during daytime, because Allied aircraft rarely attacked at night – this was due to the ASV Mk I/II radar suffering from target blackout when it came within 1,000 yards of a contact. U-boats increasingly ran surfaced across the Bay of Biscay only during night hours, remaining submerged during daylight.

On 5 June 1942, just ten weeks after sinking SS *Dixie Arrow*, *U-71* was badly damaged by depth charges dropped by a No. 10 Sqn Sunderland when its seasoned commander, Kapitänleutnant Walter Flachsenberg, decided to run surfaced for the U-boat's first 24 hours at sea at the start of its sixth patrol. Having exhausted his supply of depth charges, Flt Lt Sam Wood made repeated strafing passes at the motionless U-boat, but to no avail. Flachsenberg nursed *U-71* back to La Pallice for repairs. Although it conducted five more war patrols, the U-boat never sank another ship. (Author's Collection)

In June, aircraft equipped with Leigh Lights arrived in the front line. Paired with ASV, they made U-boats more vulnerable at night than during the day. Sunderlands were not equipped with Leigh Lights and had to drop flares for illumination, and the latter generally gave U-boats time to escape through submerging. In August, U-boats began receiving Metox radar detectors, and RAF Coastal Command crews quickly reported that radar contacts were disappearing immediately after appearing. Warned by Metox, the submarines had dived.

Since Sunderlands lacked Leigh Lights, RAF Coastal Command made a virtue of necessity. To force the U-boats to make a more time-consuming crossing of the Bay of Biscay submerged, No. 19 Group had Sunderlands fly with their radars on continuously at night. Patrols were staggered to provide almost complete radar coverage over the area, this tactic turning the flying boat into an aerial scarecrow.

TURNING POINT

As 1943 began Sunderland squadrons had become secondary in the fight against U-boats. The star players were the Leigh Light-equipped Wellingtons and Liberators, especially the latter. They carried new ASW weapons, including the Fido homing torpedo and HVARs. As the year progressed, Wellington, Liberator and Halifax squadrons were also the first to be equipped with ASV Mk III radar. It looked as if the major role for the Sunderland in 1943 was to continue to play scarecrow, broadcasting with their ASV Mk II units to force U-boats underwater. Oddly, the ASV Mk III, which Sunderlands were not yet then carrying, became one factor that returned the flying boat to the role of U-boat killer.

The U-boats were now armed with heavier anti-aircraft batteries than in 1941–42, and on 1 May 1943, Dönitz issued Standing War Order No. 483, which became known as the 'Fight Back' directive. It instructed U-boat commanders to remain submerged at night to the maximum extent possible, and when faced by an aircraft during daylight to remain surfaced and fight it out if they lacked time to dive. Previously, U-boats conducted an emergency dive under all circumstances. Dönitz believed it was worth trying to see off any attack from the air – three U-boats that had recently 'slugged it out' with RAF Coastal Command aircraft had shot down or driven off their foes.

If a U-boat wanted to fight an aircraft it was better off remaining surfaced during daylight hours, for it was easier to engage aircraft when you could see them. Metox would provide the alert, and the lookouts would spot the approaching danger long before the crew of the aircraft could engage. Thus, in 1943, Sunderlands were more likely to encounter surfaced U-boats during daylight hours than had previously been the case.

This early-build Sunderland III of No. 461 Sqn, based at Pembroke Dock, in 1943–44 lacked the fixed machine guns in the nose. The second Australian-manned Sunderland unit to serve with RAF Coastal Command, No. 461 Sqn was credited with sinking two U-boats during the Bay Campaign of 1943. (Tony Holmes Collection)

The frequency of engagements also rose simply because there were now more Sunderlands patrolling the Bay of Biscay. In early 1942 only No. 10 Sqn was routinely operating the flying boat in this area, and it was joined in the spring by No. 461 Sqn as RAF Coastal Command made its first concerted push to deny U-boats free passage through the Bay of Biscay. When this campaign recommenced in May 1943, there were five Sunderland units available – the RAF's Nos. 201 and 228 Sqns and the RCAF's No. 423 Sqn were now also assigned to No. 19 Group.

Sometimes, the U-boat won after being engaged by a flying boat. The first example of this type of encounter was the battle

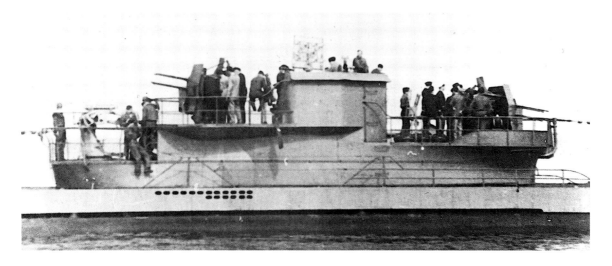

between *U-441* and a No. 228 Sqn Sunderland fought in the Bay of Biscay on 24 May 1943. By then Dönitz's 'Fight Back' order had been in effect almost a month, and six aircraft had been shot down. Flg Off H. J. Debnam, captain of the flying boat, expected the U-boat to remain surfaced as he turned in to attack. Sunderland crews had already sunk three vessels (*U-465*, *U-663* and *U-753*) that had decided to fight it out that month, and Debnam was hoping to bag a fourth.

He had found *U-441*, on its fourth war patrol. A Type VIIC boat first commissioned in February 1942, *U-441* had sunk only one ship during its career. It would not add to that total during this patrol either, for *U-441* was hunting aircraft not ships. The vessel had recently been converted into a Flak boat, with two quad 20mm cannon in armoured mounts on the 'bandstands' forward and aft of the conning tower, plus a single 37mm weapon aft. Its crew numbered 67, including a doctor to tend the wounded following an engagement with enemy aircraft. Due to increasing casualties because of air attacks, from the beginning of July 1943, 50 per cent of U-boats carried a doctor.

U-441's original commander, Kapitänleutnant Klaus Hartmann, became seriously ill in mid-May just as the vessel was ready to sail on its first Flak boat war patrol. He was replaced by Kapitänleutnant Götz von Hartmann, a veteran and aggressive U-boat skipper. In three patrols commanding Type VIIC boat *U-563*, he had sunk three ships totalling 14,689 tons and damaged two others (including a tanker) for another 16,266 tons.

Unaware of *U-441*'s conversion, Debnam turned in to attack the U-boat and was met by a wall of fire from the forward quad 20mm mount and the 37mm cannon. The Sunderland was lucky, for the aft quad 20mm mount was unserviceable following the failure of a corroded weld. Nevertheless, the flying boat was hit multiple times as it approached *U-441*. Despite suffering significant damage, the Sunderland dropped a stick of depth charges as it passed over the U-boat. One caused a hull leak and another damaged the rudder, forcing *U-441* to return to Brest for repairs. The No. 228 Sqn Sunderland subsequently crashed attempting to return to base, with the loss of all 11 crew. It was the first Sunderland to be shot down by a U-boat, and the first success credited to a Flak boat.

U-441 departs Brest at the start of its first patrol as a Flak boat on 22 May 1943. The crew succeeded in shooting down a Sunderland from No. 228 Sqn two days after this photograph was taken, but the U-boat suffered serious damage in the process. *U-441* had to return to Brest for repairs that took more than a month to complete. The 'bandstands' forward and aft of the conning tower are clearly visible, and each one has a quad mount featuring C/38 20mm cannon – this armament fit was unique to the quartet of Flak boats briefly fielded by the Kriegsmarine in 1943. (NHHC)

OPPOSITE BELOW

The gun crew run to their battle stations after being alerted to the presence of an aircraft. This photograph was taken during a drill in early 1943 onboard what appears to be a Type IX U-boat. The weapon in the foreground is a deck-mounted 37mm/69 FlaK M42, and at least two MG 42 7.92mm machine guns are visible on the conning tower. (Getty Images)

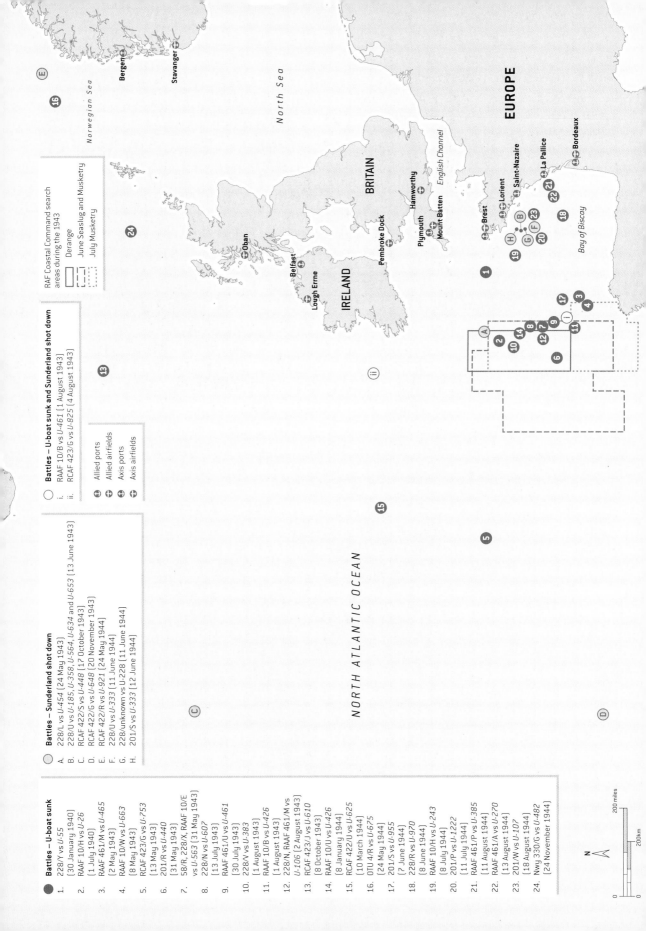

Battles – U-boat sunk

● 1. 228/Y vs *U-55*
   (30 January 1940)
2. RAAF 10/H vs *U-26*
   (1 July 1940)
3. RAAF 461/M vs *U-465*
   (2 May 1943)
4. RAAF 10/W vs *U-663*
   (8 May 1943)
5. RCAF 423/G vs *U-753*
   (13 May 1943)
6. 201/R vs *U-440*
   (31 May 1943)
7. 58/R, 228/X, RAAF 10/E
   vs *U-563* (31 May 1943)
8. 228/N vs *U-607*
   (13 July 1943)
9. RAAF 461/U vs *U-461*
   (30 July 1943)
10. 228/V vs *U-383*
   (1 August 1943)
11. RAAF 10/B vs *U-426*
   (1 August 1943)
12. 228/N, RAAF 461/M vs
   U-106 (2 August 1943)
13. RCAF 423/J vs *U-610*
   (8 October 1943)
14. RAAF 10/U vs *U-426*
   (8 January 1944)
15. RCAF 422/U vs *U-625*
   (10 March 1944)
16. OTU 4/R vs *U-675*
   (24 May 1944)
17. 201/S vs *U-955*
   (7 June 1944)
18. 228/R vs *U-970*
   (8 June 1944)
19. RAAF 10/H vs *U-243*
   (8 July 1944)
20. 201/P vs *U-1222*
   (11 July 1944)
21. RAAF 461/P vs *U-385*
   (11 August 1944)
22. RAAF 461/A vs *U-270*
   (13 August 1944)
23. 201/W vs *U-107*
   (18 August 1944)
24. Nwy 330/G vs *U-482*
   (24 November 1944)

Battles – Sunderland shot down

○ A. 228/L vs *U-54* (24 May 1943)
B. 228/U vs *U-185, U-358, U-564, U-634* and *U-653* (13 June 1943)
C. RCAF 422/S vs *U-448* (17 October 1943)
D. RCAF 422/G vs *U-648* (20 November 1943)
E. RCAF 422/R vs *U-921* (24 May 1944)
F. 228/U vs *U-333* (11 June 1944)
G. 228/unknown vs *U-228* (11 June 1944)
H. 201/S vs *U-333* (12 June 1944)

Battles – U-boat sunk and Sunderland shot down

○ RAAF 10/B vs *U-461* (1 August 1943)
RCAF 423/G vs *U-825* (4 August 1943)

Allied ports
i. Allied airfields
ii. Axis ports
Axis airfields

RAF Coastal Command search areas during the 1943
Derange
June Seaslug and Musketry
July Musketry

EUROPE
BRITAIN
IRELAND
Bergen
Stavanger
Norwegian Sea
North Sea
English Channel
Oban
Belfast
Lough Erne
Pembroke Dock
Hamworthy
Plymouth
Mount Batten
Brest
Lorient
Saint-Nazaire
La Pallice
Bordeaux
Bay of Biscay
NORTH ATLANTIC OCEAN

N
0   200km
0   200 miles

The result of this particular clash was unusual, for the Sunderland typically prevailed. An example of the latter was the sinking of *U-106* on 2 August 1943. Hoping to saturate the aircraft seeking U-boats by flooding the Bay of Biscay with vessels, Dönitz sent out seven, including *U-106*. Most were sunk, mainly by aircraft.

U-106 was a Type IXB boat with a storied career. The submarine had conducted its first war patrol in January 1941, and during the

course of nine such deployments, under the command of Kapitänleutnante Jürgen Oesten and Hermann Rasch, it sank 22 ships for a total of 138,581 tons and damaged four more totalling 51,980 tons – it ranked 20th in the list of most successful U-boats of World War II in terms of tonnage sunk.

On 2 August, *U-106*, now under the command of Oberleutnant zur see Wolf-Dietrich Damerow, was on the sixth day of its tenth patrol. Early that morning it had been attacked by aircraft, having also been targeted on the 1st. Although the U-boat had emerged unscathed from the first engagement, the second attack by a Wellington from No. 407 Sqn RCAF saw *U-106* straddled by depth charges that inflicted sufficient damage to force the vessel to head back in the direction of its home port, Lorient. Dönitz sent out three E-boats to escort the cripple.

RAF Coastal Command immediately began searching for *U-106*, and at 1620 hrs a No. 228 Sqn Sunderland spotted the three E-boats that were also looking for the crippled U-boat. When they began shooting at the flying boat, the aircraft quickly took cover in nearby clouds while simultaneously reporting the encounter. The radio transmission drew a response from two other Sunderlands – another No. 228 Sqn aircraft commanded by Flg Off Reader Hanbury and a No. 461 Sqn Sunderland with Flg Off Irwin A. F. 'Chic' Clarke as captain. They began shadowing the E-boats until a Royal Navy escort group came in to sight. By then it was 1804 hrs, and the Sunderlands left to continue their patrol.

At 1852 hrs Hanbury spotted a U-boat three miles southeast of the retiring E-boats. It was *U-106*, which was searching for its escorts. Hanbury attacked, but was met by gunfire. Damerow subsequently reported, 'A Sunderland was spotted approaching from ahead at a range of 800m, altitude medium. I opened fire on her at once, and she sheared off to starboard, circling us outside gun range'.

Trailing smoke from depth charge attacks, *U-106* is strafed by a Sunderland during the early evening of 2 August 1943 while attempting to return to Lorient. Having been damaged earlier that day by depth charges from a Wellington of No. 407 Sqn, the U-boat was finished off in a coordinated attack by Sunderlands from Nos. 228 and 461 Sqns. (Author's Collection)

ENGAGING THE ENEMY

Flak gunners on board *U-106* attempt to defend their U-boat from a coordinated attack by two Sunderlands northwest of Cape Ortegal on 8 August 1943. The twin C/38 20mm mount is firing at the flying boat from No. 461 Sqn, while the quad mount on the rear 'bandstand' has been aimed at the trailing Sunderland from No. 228 Sqn. Both weapons could put up a stout defence if the U-boat was targeted by a single aircraft, but if the vessel was unlucky enough to be attacked by multiple aerial threats, the submarine usually ended up being sunk.

Sunderland III DV980 of No. 228 Sqn sits in Milford Haven off Pembroke Bay during the summer of 1943, the unit being heavily involved in the Bay Campaign that year – it lost two flying boats and had a third damaged whilst engaging U-boats. No. 228 Sqn also lost another Sunderland to a U-boat on 11 June 1944. DV980 has four fixed 0.303-in. machine guns in the nose just beneath the turret, these weapons being fired by the pilot. (Tony Holmes Collection)

Then, at 1904 hrs, Clarke joined Hanbury. After a few minutes of circling, they launched a coordinated attack on *U-106* in an attempt to overwhelm its Flak batteries. Clarke attacked the port bow while Hanbury dived on the starboard bow. According to Damerow, 'The one to starboard is engaged by quadruple 2cm, and the one to port by the single 2cm and machine guns'. Clarke roared in at a height of just 50ft, while his bow gunner, Sgt John Royal, sprayed *U-106*'s 'bandstands' with 0.303-in. rounds that cut down the crew of the quad 20mm weapon on the 'Wintergarten' directly aft of the conning tower.

The two Sunderlands flew directly over *U-106* within seconds of each other, Clarke dropping six depth charges from a height of 50ft just 50 yards astern of the submarine. Hanbury, attacking from 100ft, perfectly straddled the vessel with seven depth charges that bracketed the conning tower. The twin attacks left *U-106* in a desperate condition. According to Damerow, Clarke's depth charges 'caused severe concussion to the boat', and Hanbury's ripped 'the port engine-room switchboard from its securings, causing it to catch fire. The starboard diesel stopped. Thick smoke filled the boat, which listed to port with a bad leak'.

Then Hanbury and Clarke wheeled around and came in for a second attack. Each Sunderland had one depth charge left, Hanbury approaching from out of the sun so as to blind the gunners. For a second time the flying boats' bow gunners silenced their counterparts defending the U-boat. Both aircraft made careful attacks with their remaining depth charges, and both weapons landed close, causing severe damage. 'The port diesel now also stopped', Damerow reported, 'and both electric motors were out of action. The boat was out of control and settled by the stern. Chlorine gas was escaping from the batteries'.

Damerow ordered that *U-106* be abandoned. As some crewmen jumped overboard, others manned the guns and continued to engage the Sunderlands. The latter responded by strafing *U-106* and killing both gunners and sailors attempting to escape. At 2015 hrs the U-boat exploded, leaving debris and the surviving crew scattered on the surface of the water. By then, Clarke, low on fuel, was on his way

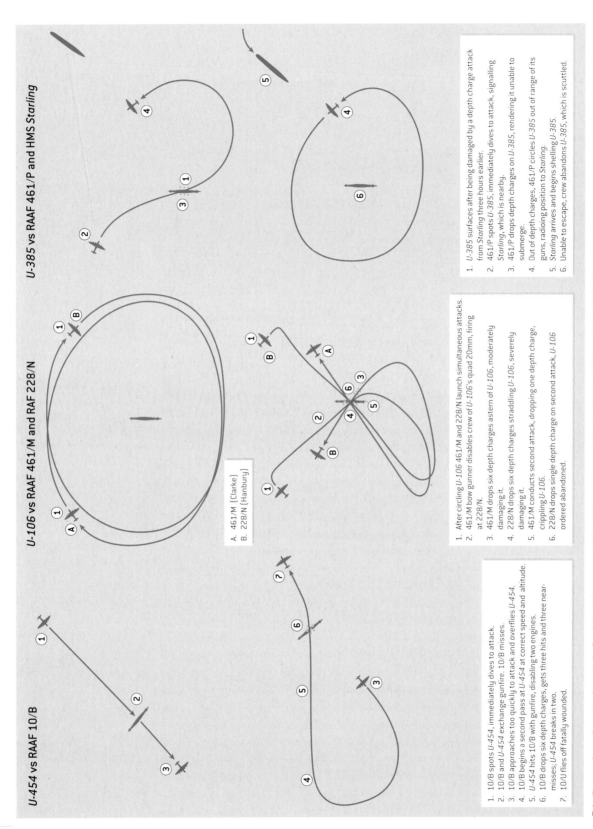

U-454 vs RAAF 10/B

1. 10/B spots U-454, immediately dives to attack.
2. 10/B and U-454 exchange gunfire. 10/B misses.
3. 10/B approaches too quickly to attack and overflies U-454.
4. 10/B begins a second pass at U-454 at correct speed and altitude.
5. U-454 hits 10/B with gunfire, disabling two engines.
6. 10/B drops six depth charges, gets three hits and three near-misses; U-454 breaks in two.
7. 10/U flies off fatally wounded.

U-106 vs RAAF 461/M and RAF 228/N

A. 461/M [Clarke]
B. 228/N [Hanburg]

1. After circling U-106 461/M and 228/N launch simultaneous attacks.
2. 461/M bow gunner disables crew of U-106's quad 20mm, firing at 228/N.
3. 461/M drops six depth charges astern of U-106, moderately damaging it.
4. 228/N drops six depth charges straddling U-106, severely damaging it.
5. 461/M conducts second attack, dropping one depth charge, crippling U-106.
6. 228/N drops single depth charge on second attack, U-106 ordered abandoned.

U-385 vs RAAF 461/P and HMS Starling

1. U-385 surfaces after being damaged by a depth charge attack from Starling three hours earlier.
2. 461/P spots U-385, immediately dives to attack, signalling Starling, which is nearby.
3. 461/P drops depth charges on U-385, rendering it unable to submerge.
4. Out of depth charges, 461/P circles U-385 out of range of its guns, radioing position to Starling.
5. Starling arrives and begins shelling U-385.
6. Unable to escape, crew abandons U-385, which is scuttled.

This diagram shows three attacks made by Sunderlands in, or near, the Bay of Biscay that resulted in the sinking of U-boats during 1943—44.

home. After observing the explosion and subsequent sinking, Hanbury followed. The E-boats picked up 36 survivors from *U-106*'s crew of 58.

Sometimes, both the hunter and the hunted were destroyed, with one such encounter occurring on 1 August 1943. *U-454* had departed La Pallice on 26 July 1943, the Type VIIC U-boat undertaking its tenth war patrol under the command of Kapitänleutnant Burckhard Hackländer – he had been *U-454*'s first and only captain. On its previous deployment, the U-boat had spent a total of 283 days at sea. To avoid enemy aircraft, Hackländer skirted south across the Bay of Biscay, almost coming in sight of the Spanish coast, before turning northeast just east of the Portuguese–Spanish border. He ran submerged on the night of 31 July, before surfacing at 0830 hrs on 1 August. Almost immediately a patrolling aircraft forced him to dive, and when he resurfaced at 1100 hrs, the same thing happened again.

By 1400 hrs, after almost 18 hours submerged, *U-454* desperately needed to recharge its batteries and refresh its air. At 1440 hrs Hackländer resurfaced, and the U-boat was almost immediately spotted by the No. 10 Sqn Sunderland commanded by Flt Lt K. G. 'Bob' Fry. Like Hackländer, Fry was a seasoned veteran – this was his 28th flight as the captain of a Sunderland. Twenty minutes earlier, he had flown past the five warships of Capt F. J. 'Johnnie' Walker's 2nd Support Group, also hunting U-boats in the western Bay of Biscay. Upon spotting the U-boat Fry dropped two flares to alert Walker of his find and turned to attack the vessel.

When lookouts spotted the Sunderland two miles off *U-454*'s port beam, Hackländer chose to fight it out on the surface. He had little choice in the matter, subsequently writing, 'The situation was now serious, the batteries were exhausted and the air was foul'. Fry was, of course, unaware of this. What he saw was a surfaced U-boat. Despite being too high, too fast and too close to make an effective attack, he tried anyway. Due to his poor positioning, and excessive altitude, Fry could not drop his depth charges as he passed over *U-454*'s bow. The U-boat had twin 20mm guns and a single 20mm weapon on separate 'bandstand' mounts aft of the conning tower, which Fry's nose gunner tried to suppress with fire from his twin 0.303-in. guns. His rounds went wide, as did those of the gun batteries on board *U-454*.

Undeterred, Fry turned for a second pass, heading towards *U-454* at minimum altitude. The gunner of the twin 20mm mount on the upper bandstand finally found the range of the Sunderland, hitting both starboard engines. The shattered starboard inner engine flew off as more hits raked the Sunderland, yet Fry somehow kept the aircraft under control and dropped six depth charges as he flew over *U-454*. It was a perfect straddle. Three hit close on either side of the vessel, while the remining three exploded on the hull itself. *U-454* broke in two and sank in 30 seconds. Thirty-two crew went down with it, although Hackländer and 13 men, all from the deck watch, were left in the water. They were rescued by the 2nd Support Group sloop *HMS Kite*.

With two engines out on one wing, the badly damaged Sunderland would never make it home. Fry turned it towards the oncoming sloops and attempted a landing in choppy seas. The flying boat bounced off two wave tops, stalled and dropped into the water, ripping off its starboard wing. HMS *Wren*, close at hand, was able to recover six survivors – the navigator, the second engineer and four gunners, all in the aft part of the Sunderland. Six others, including Fry, perished in the crash.

TO WAR'S END

The battle in the Bay of Biscay had reached its climax in 1943, when 12 U-boats were sunk in engagements involving Sunderlands. The action continued unabated during 1944, when a further 12 vessels were sunk. The clashes that year were fought in a different way to those that had occurred in 1943, with the first big change being Dönitz's abandonment of Standing War Order No. 483. The one-sided battles in the Bay of Biscay between U-boats and aircraft had demonstrated the folly of this directive. Thereafter, U-boats avoided aircraft as best they could, especially in the Bay of Biscay. They ran submerged to the greatest extent possible, and hugged the Spanish coast when crossing the area. They also avoided attacking convoys when aircraft were present. Finally, U-boat commanders were instructed to remain submerged and use Schnorchels to run their diesels whenever possible.

None of this worked, however, for there were simply too many Allied aircraft patrolling the Bay of Biscay by 1944 to allow U-boats to remain surfaced long enough to recharge their batteries. Submarines were inevitably spotted, at which point their best defence was to crash-dive and hope the aircraft ran out of fuel before the U-boat ran out of battery charge and air. Even Schnorchels did not help much, for later marks of ASV radar could spot the raised head section above the water. Worse, the noise of the diesels operating while the U-boat was submerged deafened the vessel's hydrophones, leaving the crew unable to hear an approaching Allied warship. They also made such a racket that the U-boat could be easily detected by the hydrophones of Allied warships patrolling in the area. While Schnorchels mitigated the aircraft threat, they aggravated the warship threat.

The situation reached another climax in June 1944, when the Allied landings at Normandy on the north coast of France led to one final push by U-boats in the Bay of Biscay. Dönitz sent 36 submarines – every available U-boat in French ports – to attack shipping off the Allied beachhead. The result was a massacre of U-boats in which the Sunderland participated. The flying boats had sunk four in the first five months of the year (*U-426*, *U-571*, *U-625* and *U-675*), and four more would be claimed in June–July (*U-955*, *U-970*, *U-243* and *U-1222*), three in August (*U-385*, *U-270* and *U-107*) and, finally, one in November (*U-482*). In turn, in June, with U-boats desperately seeking to break into the English Channel, nine Allied aircraft had been shot down attacking submarines, three of them Sunderlands.

Seasoned veteran Kapitänleutnant Peter-Erich 'Ali' Cremer skippered *U-333* during this period. The most experienced U-boat commander then still alive, he had led this vessel on eight of its previous ten war patrols, and was responsible for sinking more than 36,000 tons of *U-333*'s credited 41,350 tons. Although the U-boat lacked a Schnorchel on its 11th war patrol, Cremer took it out in any case on 6 June. The patrol proved to be an aircraft-induced nightmare, as Cremer later wrote. 'For *U-333* it was all over in seven days. We scarcely set foot on deck the whole time and were fully stretched fighting off aircraft'.

He spent most of the hours of darkness after midnight on 10 June diving to avoid aircraft. Finally, at 0910 hrs, low on battery charge, Cremer was forced to surface. The No. 10 Sqn Sunderland commanded by Flt Lt H. A. McGregor spotted *U-333* as it appeared, and he attacked with such speed that a number of crewmen were sent tumbling. The armourer tripped while lowering the port bomb door, jamming it. More importantly, McGregor's violent manoeuvre delayed the bow gunner's suppressive fire. This allowed *U-333*'s crew to man an anti-aircraft battery. As Cremer described, 'Like a hawk, it plunged steeply down on us from about 200m. We escaped a collision by less than 30m, then it was all over'. When McGregor tried to drop six depth charges, three hung up and three others fell astern of *U-333*. Cremer submerged again and headed for the bottom, with *U-333* shaken, but undamaged.

He remained underwater for the rest of the day, resurfacing at sunset. Despite releasing a radar decoy, *U-333* was again found by aircraft, attacked twice and forced to submerge. It resurfaced again at midnight of 12 June, and this time Cremer had no choice but to stay and fight. *U-333* was again spotted by a Sunderland, the flying boat being assigned to No. 201 Sqn and captained by Sqn Ldr W. D. B. Ruth (who had sunk *U-955* off northern Spain on 7 June). 'It came straight towards us out of the darkness at a height of about 70m, and directly into the fire of our 2-centimetre guns', Cremer wrote. 'With a single burst, our gunner hit one engine of the aircraft, which at once burst into flames and crashed'.

Kapitänleutnant Peter-Erich 'Ali' Cremer was commander of *U-333* when it survived an attack by a No. 10 Sqn Sunderland on 10 June 1944. Two days later, the U-boat was targeted by a flying boat from No. 201 Sqn, which was promptly shot down by Flak gunners. *U-333* had also shot down a Wellington from No. 172 Sqn in the Bay of Biscay on 4 March 1943. (Tony Holmes Collection)

The depth charges aboard the aircraft exploded as it hit the water, their detonation being close enough to *U-333* to cause leaks. Water dripped in and oil oozed out, creating a tell-tale slick. The buoyancy tanks and conning tower had also been damaged by 0.303-in. rounds, as the Sunderland's rear gunner had kept firing until the flying boat hit the water. The crash was witnessed by other patrolling aircraft, drawing undesired attention. Cremer turned *U-333* south, out of the interdiction zone, arriving at Lorient on 13 June. He and his had crew survived where others had not. Between 6–15 June 11 U-boats had been sunk, nine of them by aircraft. Two of the latter, the Type VIIC U-boats *U-955* (credited to Sqn Ldr W. D. B. Ruth) and *U-970*, had fallen victim to Sunderlands of Nos. 201 and 228 Sqns.

The battle for the Bay of Biscay ended in September, with the French ports frequented by U-boats being abandoned by the Kriegsmarine between 26–28 August after the Allies broke out of the Normandy beachhead. U-boats remaining in those ports were reassigned to Norwegian bases. Thereafter, Sunderlands found few U-boats in French waters, resulting in the flying boat squadrons being reassigned to strengthen patrols in the Iceland–Britain gap and in the Norwegian Sea. Just as in 1942, crews found a shortage of targets, with the last U-boat to be sunk due to the involvement of a Sunderland being *U-482* west of the Shetland Islands on 25 November. Although destruction of the vessel was credited to the frigate HMS *Ascension*, *U-482* had initially been detected by a Sunderland from Norwegian-manned No. 330 Sqn.

STATISTICS AND ANALYSIS

There were thousands of encounters between Sunderlands and U-boats during World War II. The vast majority were simple sightings, generally by U-boats of aircraft, including Sunderlands. Perhaps a quarter of those sightings developed into an actual attack on a U-boat by a Sunderland. Of those, less than ten per cent led to damage to either the U-boat or the flying boat. Only 35 led to fatal damage being inflicted on a U-boat, a Sunderland or both.

There were several reasons for this relatively low total. For much of the war, German crews usually submerged upon sighting an aircraft, rather than staying on the surface to determine whether it was a friend or foe. As Kapitänleutnant Peter Cremer observed in his memoirs, 'it was not the task of U-boats to shoot down aircraft, but to avoid them'. Between September 1939 and April 1943 U-boats actively avoided Sunderlands, fighting them only when forced to. Only between May and September 1943 did U-boat crews routinely take the fight to Allied aircraft, with a subsequent increase in vessels sunk or damaged and aircraft shot down.

Another reason was that Britain lacked effective ASW weapons for aircraft for the first 18 months of the war. The 100lb and 250lb anti-submarine bombs were worthless, and there were too few Mk VII depth charges for Sunderlands to routinely carry them. The two U-boat 'kills' credited to Sunderlands in 1940 were the result of crews scuttling their boats after being attacked with anti-submarine bombs. Their demise had more to do with previous damage, and the knowledge there were Royal Navy warships nearby being directed to the crippled U-boats by Sunderlands.

Flying boat crews also lacked key tools to locate and sink U-boats until 1941, when the U-boat-killing Mk VIII depth charge became available. And although they were the first radar-equipped RAF Coastal Command aircraft, Sunderlands initially carried ASV Mk I/II radar, which, crucially, lost resolution at attack range. This meant that Sunderland crews would only be able to achieve kills using radar *if* they could visually spot their quarry. In 1941–42 U-boats primarily surfaced at night only.

Sunderlands were never equipped with Leigh Lights, requiring them to illuminate U-boats with flares. This meant two passes, giving U-boats time to submerge. It was possible to sink a U-boat which had just submerged, and a No. 10 Sqn Sunderland did exactly that on 10 September 1941 when it targeted the Italian submarine *Alessandro Malaspina* in the Bay of Biscay. It required luck, and Sunderland crews were only lucky that one time prior to 1943.

Nor did the Sunderlands directly benefit from the development of ASV Mk III radar, as they retained the less capable ASV Mk II through much of 1943. Sunderlands finally received ASV Mk III and later models later that year, allowing the night attack experienced by *U-333* in June 1944.

It took Standing War Order No. 483, in addition to ASV Mk III, to make the Sunderland a U-boat killer once again. ASV Mk III meant U-boats were better off attempting to cross the Bay of Biscay surfaced during the day, when Sunderlands could see and attack them. The 'Fight Back' order kept them on the surface, allowing Sunderlands to attack. By the time Dönitz abandoned the order in late 1943,

A senior officer (possibly Korvettenkapitän Herbert Sohler, commander of *7. Flotille*) addresses the crews from two U-boats probably in the French port of Saint-Nazaire in March 1943 before the vessels head out into the now dangerous waters of the Bay of Biscay, bound for the North Atlantic. Both U-boats are Type VIIs, and they appear to be very lightly armed in respect to anti-aircraft weapons. (Getty Images)

ASV Mk III-equipped Sunderlands were appearing. Even without ASV Mk III, the Sunderland would have been effective, as U-boats continued to cross the Bay of Biscay surfaced during the day. The Kriegsmarine had mistakenly abandoned Metox in August 1943, thus leaving them blind to approaching ASV Mk II-equipped Sunderlands, and they did not begin installing Naxos, capable of detecting ASV Mk III transmissions, until late September 1943.

The combination of these factors meant that 1943–44 was the Sunderland's most productive period for sinking U-boats – they assisted in the destruction of two in 1940, after which the best part of three years would pass before Sunderlands sank or assisted in sinking 24 U-boats in 1943–44. Of these, 19 were in or immediately adjacent to the Bay of Biscay, including nine of 12 kills in 1943 and eight of 12 kills in 1944. All but one of the rest were sunk in the gap between Iceland and Britain (the final sinking was off the Norwegian coast).

The success of the D-Day landings in June 1944 eventually spelled the end for U-boat operations in the Bay of Biscay. With the abandonment of the French ports, the Bay of Biscay was left devoid of U-boats. The latter had also ceased their attacks on North Atlantic convoys, which meant fewer U-boats transiting through areas patrolled by Sunderlands. No more U-boats were sunk by Sunderlands after 25 November 1944.

Although the Sunderland fought U-boats over a longer period than any other RAF Coastal Command type, they were not the deadliest aircraft U-boats faced. That title went to the Liberator, whose crews sank or contributed to the sinking of 72 U-boats. This was more than the combined totals of the second-place Catalina (40) and third-place Wellington (27) combined. All three aircraft types exceeding the Sunderland's total were equipped with Leigh Lights – an advantage the Sunderland lacked. They could also carry homing torpedoes.

U-boats fared worse against aircraft than aircraft did against U-boats. Over the course of the war, U-boats shot down 110 aircraft of all types – this total excludes at least six aircraft brought down by their own bombs while attacking U-boats. Of these, 93 were multi-engined patrol aircraft. Most shoot-downs occurred from 1943 through to VE Day, U-boats having destroyed just eight aircraft prior to January of that year. U-bootsmanner had no motivation to fight aircraft in the war's early years. During that period, putting a few feet of water between a U-boat and the surface made it virtually invulnerable to aircraft attack. Staying surfaced and fighting was stupid. Even after RAF Coastal Command got Mk VIII depth charges, it was largely luck if a U-boat was hit once it had submerged. Additionally, there were relatively few aircraft seeking U-boats.

In 1943 the Allies finally committed enough aircraft to saturate the areas where U-boats were operating, especially the Bay of Biscay and the Iceland–Britain gap. Coinciding with the issuing of Standing War Order No. 483, frequent 'shoot-outs' between aircraft and U-boats subsequently occurred. By the time Dönitz discontinued the order, the Allies had so many patrol aircraft available they could cover virtually every mile of the Bay of Biscay.

This led to the situation Kapitänleutnant Cremer described when he shot down a No. 228 Sqn Sunderland the day after his vessel had been targeted by a flying boat from No. 10 Sqn. That paled when compared to the nightmare voyage experienced

by *U-415* during the same period. Its skipper, Oberleutnant zur See Herbert Werner, described the patrol, which started from Lorient at midnight on 7 June 1944. With his U-boat having been damaged during an attack by a Wellington at 0202 hrs, Werner recalled that at '0220 hrs – impulses [on the Naxos radar detection system] now from starboard. I presumed several planes were approaching. Suddenly, a Sunderland shot out of the night from starboard ahead'.

The flying boat attacked from ahead, where *U-415*'s 20mm cannon could not bear because of its location behind the conning tower, and dropped four depth charges. The aircraft was then joined by a Liberator that bracketed *U-415*. A few minutes later, at 0228 hrs, 'Increasing engine noise heralded a new attack – a fresh approach by a Sunderland from starboard ahead, guns blazing. Zooming over our bridge, it dropped four canisters'. The attacks left *U-415* crippled, although its Flak gunners had in turn downed a Liberator from No. 224 Sqn. It was a typical U-boat encounter for this period.

Of 93 multi-engined aircraft shot down by U-boats, nine were Sunderlands – all in 1943–44. That was a ratio of 2.89 U-boats lost for every Sunderland shot down. The ratio of total U-boats lost to Sunderland attacks versus total Sunderland combat losses was much lower. The main combat threat to Sunderlands were long-range enemy fighter aircraft, not U-boats.

Some 211 U-boats were sunk by aircraft or a combination of aircraft and warships, while U-boats shot down 110 aircraft – a ratio of 1.92-to-1. While U-boats were more successful against Sunderlands than aircraft in general, Sunderland losses were consistent with other multi-engined maritime patrol aircraft.

By the time these Sunderland Vs reached No. 201 Sqn in February 1945, the U-boat threat in the Bay of Biscay had gone. In fact, the unit had been posted to Castle Archdale, in Northern Ireland, from Pembroke Dock in November 1944 due to the lack of action off the French Atlantic coast. Powered by American Pratt & Whitney R-1830 Twin Wasp engines and featuring ASV Mk VIc radar in underwing blisters (clearly visible here), the Mk V remained in service with No. 201 Sqn until February 1957. (Tony Holmes Collection)

When a U-boat did surface in the Bay of Biscay in 1943–44, it was almost inevitably attacked. This unidentified vessel, bracketed by depth charges dropped by a Sunderland, is blowing its bow tanks in a desperate attempt to keep from sinking. (Author's Collection)

The Liberator–U-boat victory-to-loss ratio was 72 to 24 (3-to-1), the Catalina's was 40 to six (6.67-to-1) and the Wellington's was 27 to 20 (1.35-to-1).

Considering the relative cost of U-boats compared to aircraft, that rate of exchange was highly unfavourable to the Kriegsmarine. U-boats needed to shoot down five to six Sunderlands to achieve parity in personnel losses. They would have had to down 12 or more to equal the cost and material involved in building one U-boat. That was unachievable. As Cremer observed, U-boats had no business fighting aircraft. They needed to avoid them.

What the duels between U-boats and Sunderlands demonstrated was that the pre-war conventional wisdom about defeating the submarine threat was correct. ASDIC, convoys and especially aircraft had made U-boats obsolete as a tool of commerce raiding. Aircraft patrolling convoys eliminated the *Rudeltaktik*'s effectiveness. That was demonstrated as early as December 1941, when aircraft embarked in the Royal Navy's first escort carrier, HMS *Audacity*, and long-range Liberators combined to cause the Kriegsmarine to lose almost twice as many U-boats as ships sunk during convoy HG 76.

Using patrol aircraft to cover the areas crossed by U-boats to get to convoys proved equally as effective for RAF Coastal Command. By the start of 1944, it had 240 aircraft (including 35 Sunderlands) patrolling the Bay of Biscay. This was enough to force U-boats to cross these now dangerous waters submerged, and risk attack every time they surfaced. The Sunderland was well suited to this duty, and, despite limitations, proved to be one of the war's most effective U-boat predators.

AFTERMATH

In some ways the RAF's stubborn refusal to properly attend to its anti-submarine responsibilities until late 1942 may have actually contributed to the eventual Allied victory over the U-boat threat. The Kriegsmarine's early successes with its submarine force led Germany to vastly expand U-boat construction. It poured resources and manpower into a force that was easily destroyed once the Allies focused on that job. The steel, men and munitions used to construct hundreds of U-boats was unavailable for other purposes.

The construction of one such vessel consumed enough steel to produce almost a battalion's worth of tanks. The pursuit of Dönitz's unwinnable tonnage war meant the Wehrmacht began Operation *Barbarossa* (the invasion of the USSR, on 22 June 1941) with fewer tanks than it could have had. Considering how close-run the Battle of Moscow and the siege of Leningrad were, perhaps we should be grateful for Air Chief Marshal Sir Arthur Harris's intransigence. When the crisis point was reached in the Battle of the Atlantic, the Allies had a solution – reallocate a few hundred available multi-engined aircraft from strategic bombing to maritime patrol. This turned the Battle of the Atlantic around in two months.

And once it was won, it stayed won. The Allies had too big a technical and material edge on the Axis. They could build patrol aircraft faster than Germany could build U-boats, and sink U-boats faster than Germany could commission them. By war's end, the Allies had tools in place to overcome Schnorchels and Elektroboots. The Sunderland was also keeping pace, being equipped with Magnetic Anomaly Detectors and the latest ASV radar.

The surviving Type VII and Type IX U-boats quickly disappeared after the war ended. Most were scuttled, many off Northern Ireland. A few were handed over to Allied countries, and the US scrapped those it received through surrender, only

The boarding party from the destroyer escort USS *Pillsbury* (DE-133) work to secure a tow line to the bow of the captured *U-505* off French Morocco on 4 June 1944. Note the large US flag flying from the U-boat's periscope. A veteran of 12 patrols between January 1942 and June 1944, the Type IXC vessel has been displayed at the Museum of Science and Industry in Chicago, Illinois, since September 1954. (NHHC)

retaining *U-505* – a war prize captured by the US Navy off French Morocco in June 1944. France, Norway and the Soviet Union commissioned submarines based on late-war U-boat designs, and these served on into the late 1960s.

The Sunderland fared a little better, and examples soldiered on after World War II with the RAF, RAAF, RNZAF, South African Air Force and the French *Aéronavale*. They took part in the Berlin Airlift (often carrying salt, as they were protected from corrosion) in 1948–49, and three RAF Sunderland squadrons participated in the Korean War. While the RAF quickly removed them from service over the Atlantic, it retained Sunderlands in the Pacific, where facilities and runways for more modern maritime patrol aircraft were scarce. The RAF retired its last military Sunderland (in Singapore) in 1959, the *Aéronavale* in 1960 and New Zealand in 1967.

That was not the end of the story, for more than 50 Sunderlands were converted into Hythe and Sandringham civil airliners and a number of them remained in commercial service well into the 1970s. Today, there is still one airworthy Sunderland (although it has not flown since 1996) and five on static display. That is a better survival rate than for U-boats. Besides *U-505*, only Type VIIC/41 *U-995* and Type IXC/40 *U-534* still exist as museum ships.

FURTHER READING

Ashworth, Chris, *RAF Coastal Command 1936–1939* (Patrick Stephens Limited, 1992)

Blair, Clay Jr., *Hitler's U-boat War – The Hunters, 1939–1942* (Random House, 1992)

Blair, Clay Jr., *Hitler's U-boat War – The Hunted, 1942–1945* (Random House, 1992)

Bowyer, Chaz, *Sunderland at War* (Ian Allen, 1994)

Cooper, Anthony, *Sub Hunters – Australian Sunderland Squadrons in the Defeat of Hitler's U-boat Menace 1942–43* (Fonthill Media, 2021)

Cremer, Peter, *U-Boat Commander – A Periscope View of the Battle of the Atlantic* (Naval Institute Press, 1984)

Franks, Norman, *Conflict over the Bay – Momentous Battles Fought by RAF and American Aircraft Against the U-boats, Bay of Biscay May–August 1943* (William Kimber, 1986)

Hendrie, Andrew, *The Cinderella Service – RAF Coastal Command 1939–1945* (Pen & Sword, 2006)

Meier, Friedrich, *Kriegsmarine am Feind* (Verlag Erich Klingmammer, 1940)

Quaife, John, *The Australian Air Campaign, Series 3 – Battle of the Atlantic – RAAF in Coastal Command 1939–45* (Big Sky Publishing, 2022)

Richards, Denis, *The Royal Air Force 1939–1945, Vol 1 – The Fight at Odds* (Her Majesty's Stationary Office, 1953)

Richards, Denis and Saunders, Hilary St. George, *The Royal Air Force 1939–1945, Volume II – The Fight Avails* (Her Majesty's Stationary Office, 1954)

Saunders, Hilary St. George, *The Royal Air Force 1939–1945, Volume III – The Fight Is Won* (Her Majesty's Stationary Office, 1954)

Werner, Herbert, *Iron Coffins – A U-boat Commander's War, 1939–1945* (Cassell & Co, 1969)

Williamson, Gordon, *Osprey Warrior 37 – German Seaman 1939–45* (Osprey Publishing, 2009)

INDEX